WELL-HEELED

Lesley-Anne Scorgie

WELL-HEELED

The $mart Girl's Guide to Getting RICH

DUNDURN
TORONTO

Project Editor: Carrie Gleason
Copy Editor: Beth McAuley
Illustrator: Natalie Catania
Design: Jesse Hooper
Printer: Webcom

Library and Archives Canada Cataloguing in Publication

Scorgie, Lesley, author
        Well-heeled : the smart girl's guide to getting rich / Lesley-Anne Scorgie.

Includes index.
Issued in print and electronic formats.
ISBN 978-1-4597-2354-2 (pbk.).--ISBN 978-1-4597-2428-0 (pdf).--ISBN 978-1-4597-2429-7 (epub)

1. Women--Finance, Personal. 2. Wealth. 3. Success. I. Title.

HG179 S3538 2014   332.0240082   C2014-901007-9
                                           C2014-901008-7

1   2   3   4   5   18   17   16   15   14

 Conseil des Arts Canada Council
du Canada   for the Arts   Canada   ONTARIO ARTS COUNCIL
CONSEIL DES ARTS DE L'ONTARIO

We acknowledge the support of the Canada Council for the Arts and the Ontario Arts Council for our publishing program. We also acknowledge the financial support of the Government of Canada through the Canada Book Fund and Livres Canada Books, and the Government of Ontario through the Ontario Book Publishing Tax Credit and the Ontario Media Development Corporation.

Visit us at
Dundurn.com | @dundurnpress | Facebook.com/dundurnpress | Pinterest.com/dundurnpress

Dundurn   Gazelle Book Services Limited   Dundurn
3 Church Street, Suite 500   White Cross Mills   2250 Military Road
Toronto, Ontario, Canada   High Town, Lancaster, England   Tonawanda, NY
M5E 1M2   L41 4XS   U.S.A. 14150

This book is dedicated to my witty, bright, beautiful, and well-heeled big sister, Alison. As young as I can remember, I've followed after your inspiration to turn big dreams into reality. May your zest for life continue to flourish and be the glue that binds you to a lifetime of happiness.

CONTENTS

ACKNOWLEDGEMENTS

Who do you thank when being blessed with so many people you love and are forever grateful to have in your life?

To the members of my family and my dear friends — your enduring support for my passion to improve financial literacy is beyond words of gratitude. Thank you.

Thank you to Dundurn Press for the incredible opportunity to publish *Well-Heeled* and inspire young women worldwide to create a financially successful future for themselves, their families, their places of work, and their communities.

Thank you to Transatlantic Literary Agency for your tremendous efforts in refining the concept for *Well-Heeled*.

To my editors and communications, marketing, sales, and PR advisors, thank you for your valuable guidance and stewardship in building the momentum for *Well-Heeled*.

To my illustrator, Natalie Catania, thank you for transforming my words into beautiful pieces of art throughout *Well-Heeled*.

To my readers — thank you for continuing to influence and inspire my writing. Without you and your support, *Well-Heeled*, wouldn't be possible. Happy saving!

INTRODUCTION

Whether you're financially maxed out or rollin' in hundred-dollar bills, ladies, this book is for you.

Money plays a massive role in our lives. Having money will open doors and give you greater options than if you are without.

Unlike in our mothers' era, today's generation of 20- and 30-something young women are financially empowered and have embraced independence, pursuing and excelling at education, building careers, choosing healthy relationships, raising families, travelling, and buying homes, cars, investments, and wardrobes.

We have the ability to transform our money into long-term financial security *and* still have room in our budgets to celebrate our accomplishments, whether through frugal indulgences, like savouring alone-time, or more expensive ones, like making a charitable donation, buying a new pair of shoes, or taking off for a girls' weekend to New York City.

The key to balancing life's competing financial priorities — namely, our needs versus our wants — is to know how to manage money wisely and avoid common financial traps like overspending and debt. Boosting your financial knowledge will unlock your

ability to create an incredibly successful and liberating financial future. And *yes*, the future is expensive! Just think about what home ownership, further education, travel, owning a business, raising a family, and eventual retirement adds up to. But with savvy financial choices now, you can afford your future.

Having money provides us with greater choices in life, and that's important.

Picture this: you save for five years, and at the age of 30, you have enough for a down payment for your own condominium. Goodbye, roommates! Or you work your tail off for 30 years and can comfortably retire at age 55. Hello, freedom! Or maybe you're keen to change career paths and can use your savings to upgrade your education. Or perhaps your hockey-loving child has the potential to go pro, and you can afford to support the required training.

On the contrary, when you don't have money, your choices are limited, which causes stress and uncertainty, forcing you to accept your circumstances instead of being able to choose them. Now picture this: you long to be a homeowner, but are still renting at 50 years old. Or you turn 65, knowing you can't retire for another decade. Imagine being stuck in a low-paying, dead-end job, without the financial resources to retrain for a better role, or never being able to afford to put your child in extracurricular activities, let alone pursue some of your own interests. In these instances, beyond being miserable, you're vulnerable.

But this doesn't have to be your reality.

Today, you have the opportunity to earn your own money and create a life that supports your dreams. And you do not have to be a financial genius to get ahead. As of this moment, the greatest financial asset you own is knowledge. *Well-Heeled* gives you the skills to make smart financial decisions that will increase your choices, empower you to pursue your dreams, and prepare you to handle the price tags associated with your passions.

We all come from diverse monetary backgrounds, but it doesn't matter what your bank account balance is; it's what you do with it that counts!

This is your life. What do you want it to look like?

I AM NOT YOUR FATHER'S STOCKBROKER – I'M SOMETHING ELSE ENTIRELY

I'm a 30-year-old woman with a passion for improving financial literacy around the world. I've spent over a decade studying personal finance and have developed a unique approach to building wealth and helping people reach their full financial potential. I've spoken about my passion on *The Oprah Winfrey Show* and written two bestselling books, *Rich by Thirty: A Young Adult's Guide to Financial Success* (2007), and *Rich by 40: A Young Couple's Guide to Building Net Worth* (2010). Both books are dedicated to empowering young people to take control of their finances.

I wasn't born with financial knowledge, and my parents certainly weren't experts. At an early age, I simply latched on to the idea of saving for a rainy day and thought I should share my experiences with others.

Years later, my savings habits have paid off, as I've tackled tuition bills for university, bought my first home, started a small business, travelled to exciting destinations, and planned for retirement.

A FRUGAL UPBRINGING

I was born in Toronto in 1983 into a hard-working middle-class family. When I was seven years old, and my parents didn't have two nickels to rub together, our family moved west so that my mother and father could pursue their education and retrain for new professions.

Money was scarce, and for nearly a decade my family lived at the poverty line. But through part-time jobs and generous family members, my parents kept a roof over our heads, food on the table, and their tuition bills paid.

Our household thrived on frugality out of sheer necessity. My brother, sister, and I relied on second-hand stores for our bicycles, clothing, school supplies, and toys. We entertained ourselves for free with books and videos from the library, sold lemonade on hot summer days, volunteered at charitable organizations, and helped my mother clip coupons. And, like many children, I grew up reading, hiking, exploring, playing sports, making friends, and using my imagination.

My family "lived lean," which taught me to appreciate money, to never pay full price for anything, and to stretch every dollar. Though we lacked material things, we still had love, and that's what made my childhood magical.

TRANSFORMING FEAR INTO SAVINGS

It scared me to watch my stressed-out parents struggle financially and never have any options. So, at age 10, I made it my mission to find ways to earn my own money, to save it, and to grow it.

I purchased my first hundred-dollar government savings bond at 10 years old. I had received the money from my grandparents for my birthday and consulted my mother about what I could do with it. Sure, I could have bought a bicycle, but when she explained that through compounded interest and reinvested returns, my $100 would turn into $135 seven years down the road, I was hooked on saving. That same month I picked up a local flyer route and started babysitting. Before long, I'd saved another $100 and bought my bicycle, which had finally gone on sale. It was then that I realized I could have the things I wanted *and* save simultaneously.

With guidance from my parents and teachers, and by earning my own money from part-time jobs, I purchased more bonds every year after that, then mutual funds and stocks.

THE OPRAH EFFECT

Saving money became my hobby, and in grade 12, after helping teach a "Money 101" class to my peers, my financial savvy caught the attention of the local newspaper. The reporter published a front-page article entitled "Whiz Kid." The publication was syndicated across North America and discovered by a producer at *The Oprah Winfrey Show*. In February 2001, at age 17, I was a guest on the show themed "Ordinary People, Extraordinary Wealth." I was the youngest guest by more than 20 years, and my role was to talk about the importance of financial literacy for young people.

Being on *The Oprah Winfrey Show* changed my life. Oprah believed in me when I was young, and because of her encouragement, I've been able to build a career doing what I'm passionate about: promoting financial literacy.

LIFE AFTER *OPRAH*

Since appearing on the program, I have written and published two bestselling books that cover such topics as basic savings strategies, debt management (and reduction), simple investment techniques, money and relationships, paying for "big-ticket" items like homes, raising (and financing) a family, and more.

Over the past decade, I've pursued formal education in finance and developed an exciting personal brand, my own website (*www.lesleyscorgie.com*), and a popular blog. I've made appearances on numerous television programs, including *The Montel Williams Show*, *MTV Live*, and local and national news programs throughout the United States and Canada. I've written financial columns for *Metro News*, the *Globe and Mail*, *Men's Health* magazine, *Unlimited* magazine, the *Toronto Star*, and the *Calgary Herald*. And I own and operate Rich By Inc., a financial consulting company dedicated to providing financial education, resources, and tools to a variety of demographics.

I've delivered hundreds of financial literacy presentations to thousands of children, parents, singles, couples, grandparents, entrepreneurs, and business people across North America. I've been a spokesperson for Canada Savings Bonds, BMO Bank of Montreal, and the University of Alberta. When I'm not writing and speaking about saving money, I work as a financial analyst in the energy industry.

I am proud to be active in my community. My volunteer hours and donor dollars go toward uplifting women and girls through education, advocacy, and support at critical turning points in their lives.

STRIKING A BALANCE

I swear I'm totally normal. I have a job, live in a hip condo in Calgary, Alberta, and my shoe collection makes me smile. I work hard at growing my nest egg, balancing my personal life with my professional one, affording my home, and pursuing my passions. I care deeply about my relationships and have been blessed with a supportive partner, family, and friends. I enjoy travelling around the world, experiencing new things, reading, exercising, and socializing.

What's unique about my experience, compared to most young women, is that I started saving earlier.

NO FEAR

Early on, my motivation to save money was based on fear — fear that I'd end up broke, just like my parents. But today my motivation to save is having the opportunity to follow my dreams, knowing that my dreams can change throughout my life. Having money isn't about accumulating more stuff. It's about creating options.

I've experienced first-hand how making positive financial choices early can pay off monetarily, personally, and professionally by providing increased and better quality options. Today I'm in a financial position where I'm not reliant on a paycheque and can afford to "retire" in a few short years ... not that I would, because I *love* my work. But I could if I wanted to. I've got the freedom to choose.

Having the freedom to choose what I want to do and how I want to do it empowers me to make the best decisions for my life. I'm not reliant on anyone but myself, and I get to call 100 percent of the shots when it comes to choices that affect me.

WHY CARE ABOUT YOUNG WOMEN?

I am passionate about promoting financial literacy for young women because financial knowledge gives a young woman the freedom to make positive choices and pursue her dreams. Research shows that, because of her inherent biological nature to be risk-averse and community-minded, a young woman who knows how to manage money makes solid financial decisions — often better ones than her male counterparts would make.

Sadly, and for a lot of silly reasons, our society doesn't emphasize passing on financial skills to young women. Rather, mainstream media, magazines, and retailers tell us we need to spend all our money on their products. This is destructive. Picking up this book is your first step toward changing this systemic issue and unlocking your full financial potential.

IT'S YOUR CALL

Wherever you're at financially, I can guarantee that you're not broke. *Broke* is when you have nothing — zilch. You've got serious assets: you're intelligent, keen, and hard-working. By the end of *Well-Heeled*, you will have the knowledge and skills to break unhealthy financial habits and create a financial future that supports your dreams.

You don't have to be a financial guru to save money and improve your life. Even people like Warren Buffett and Suze Orman had to learn the craft. And you won't have to sacrifice your happiness for the sake of a dollar, either. *Well-Heeled* is about learning to celebrate our lives in affordable ways.

Through a balanced approach to managing money, spending wisely, earning more, saving for the future, and giving back, you can create a state of mind in which you have the flexibility to build the rich life you want — hopefully, that life includes tremendous happiness. You define *richness*.

Rich could mean selling T-shirts on a beach in Thailand with $20,000 to your name, or retiring young in your hometown with zero debt and a $2-million bank balance. There is no right answer when it comes to planning for your future. It's *your* future. Created by you. You choose your path.

PILLARS OF YOUR SUCCESSFUL FUTURE

Think of your life as having three main pillars: your personal life, your professional life, and your finances. When aligned, these pillars produce the support you need to create an awesome future for yourself. But when one of these pillars is out of balance, the roof that rests upon the three — your future — becomes unstable and has the potential to collapse. For example, perhaps you've neglected your partner in favour of advancing up the corporate ladder. Your job promotion would strengthen your finances and career path, but weaken your intimate relationship. If your partner chooses to leave, there will be a gaping hole in the pillar of your personal life, destabilizing your future and bringing you great unhappiness in the process.

Think of it another way. When the pillar of your personal life is strong — i.e., you've surrounded yourself with supportive people and have a healthy level of self-esteem — you'll generate a positive and uplifting environment in which you can thrive. A by-product of thriving personally is feeling motivated both professionally and financially, ultimately strengthening those pillars, too.

Well-Heeled isn't just about strengthening your personal finances; it's also about aligning and striking a balance between your personal and professional goals so that you can create a "rich" and fulfilling future.

WHAT YOU'LL FIND IN *WELL-HEELED*

Well-Heeled will give you the skills to create wealth through a balance of approaches to savvy spending, making more money, saving, and giving. This book will walk you through tips to tame overspending, which is the root of debt (when you pay for the past rather than invest in the future — a costly endeavour). It promotes frugal living by learning how to mind your dollars and cents through planning ahead and creating budgets that are not restrictive and boring. By being resourceful and developing greater financial confidence, you will learn how to pump up your cash flow and even get a raise. Discussions on relationships will reveal how closely linked money and relationships truly are. Setting a proper financial foundation will equip you with the tools you need to leverage your unique personal characteristics as you start saving for your future.

Well-Heeled is practical advice for young women, written by a young woman who has proven how empowering financial knowledge can be.

Well-Heeled isn't meant to change who you are as a person. It's about being yourself and maximizing your strengths to create a brilliant financial future, making you the ultimate catch — for *you*, not anyone else.

You have the power to do, be, and have whatever you want in life. So if you're ready to create an awesome future for yourself, *Well-Heeled* is for you!

Enjoy the read!

CHAPTER 1
Confessions of an Indebted Shopaholic

CONFESSION

There she was, sitting with a potential client, tense with anticipation. Sheryl sipped on her glass of Chardonnay, taking in the ambience of the hip San Francisco restaurant. At 39 years old, Sheryl was working on one of her biggest deals yet. She leaned closer to hear Pete, the marketing manager of the local theatre production company, describe what he needed in a new website. Making mental notes about Pete's needs, Sheryl asked clarifying questions, and made her pitch for the business. The bill arrived as Sheryl concluded her pitch. She quickly handed over her credit card, waving Pete off in an *I'll-take-care-of-it* fashion. The server returned a few minutes later with a sour look on his face.

"Miss, your card has been declined."

Sheryl was embarrassed and horrified. After showcasing her competence in website design, demonstrating her understanding of Pete's needs, and feeling the chemistry between her and the potential client, she was minutes away from closing a

new deal. The last thing on Sheryl's mind at that particular moment was her credit card being declined.

But Sheryl's excellent pitch for Pete's business was all for naught. Pete ended up paying the tab and concluded their evening with a "Sheryl, we'll be in touch." Judging by Pete's dismissive demeanour, she knew the opportunity to win his business was gone.

Sheryl returned to her hotel room in total disappointment. She flopped down on her bed, kicked off her pink Jessica Simpson shoes, removed her sparkly Michael Kors watch, and powered down her iPad mini. She dreaded the thought of returning home to Vancouver empty-handed the following day, where her business partner waited.

Sheryl's $800 exciting personal shopping adventure from the previous day, combined with a high existing balance on her credit card (a result of many such spending sprees), had put her over the top of her credit limit and cost her $14,000 in new business.

THE HUMOUR AND THE REALITY

Can someone please tell me why our society thinks being a shopaholic is funny? We watch movies about shopaholics. We read books about shopaholics. We think shopaholism is cute. Rather than expressing concern, we laugh when our friends return from their lunch breaks with bags of goodies, having spent hundreds of dollars in less than an hour. What's worse is that most young women who are self-proclaimed shopaholics, including Sheryl from the story above, cannot afford their purchases. Their go-to method of payment is the credit card, and their purchases cost upward of 18 percent in interest on balances carried forward.

When the thrill of the new computer, latest bag, or department-store sale wears off, the shopaholic is left with massive bills to pay and zero financial flexibility to do what she really wants, let alone build her savings. In reality, shopaholism is no less of an addiction than alcoholism, smoking, or drug abuse.

Shopaholics overspend, which leads to debt, and debt causes stress. Stress affects our sleep, relationships, and overall health. Debt is also the number-one cause of separation and divorce in North America.

Debt is powerful and dangerous when it's not managed carefully and eliminated quickly. It's a ball and chain around a young woman's ankle. It holds her back from being able to live a better life and pursue her dreams.

Despite our hope for a childhood fairy-tale ending, the stark reality is that most of us are not going to be financially bailed out by a dashing millionaire, our parents, or the local lottery.

SHOPAHOLICS AND THE GLOBAL FINANCIAL CRISIS

On a much larger scale, extremely high levels of risky debt (personal and corporate), combined with greed and poor fiscal controls, led to the recent financial crisis of 2008 and 2009.

Though it's convenient to point a finger of blame, don't kid yourself. Wall Street wasn't alone in creating this mess; shopaholics contributed to the financial crisis, too.

For many years prior to the financial crisis, while the market and real estate prices soared, shopaholics amassed obscenely high levels of consumer and mortgage debt, believing that they would continue to have iron-clad job security, home-value appreciation, and investment-account growth. So, many put themselves at financial risk to make consumer purchases such as cars and trips, bought second or third properties, and signed up for high-risk mortgages, and when home values didn't increase any more and the financial markets tanked, they were left with large loans, deflated investment accounts, and a sinking real estate market. Many people were in a negative equity position, where their home was worth less than the amount of their mortgage.

Meanwhile, on Wall Street, investment bankers were capitalizing on opportunities to repackage high-risk mortgage-backed securities to be sold to average investors. Traditionally, mortgage-backed securities aren't considered to be high risk. But the sub-prime mortgages that were bundled therein made these securities high risk without many investors realizing they were invested in speculative securities.

When the markets turned unfavourable, banks demanded that their clients, both households and businesses, return their loans and reduce their credit exposure. But because so many consumers and businesses were financially maxed out, and because so many people had lost their jobs and had minimal home equity, many couldn't afford to pay up, which led to high bankruptcy and foreclosure rates. Financial institutions involved in high-risk mortgage-backed securities, such as Bear Stearns and Lehman Brothers, lost massive amounts of money and crumbled.

Even today we are still feeling the impact of that financial catastrophe with high global and local unemployment, depressed home values, government cutbacks to important social and health programs, severely degraded savings plans, and weak investment performance.

Bright young women like ourselves can clearly see, not only for own personal financial well-being but for that of North America, that we can choose a smarter path.

FROM BAD TO BROKE

Further compounding the issue of shopaholism, many young women end up broke and indebted as a result of these additional factors:

- Because of limited training in schools and at home, many young women are not financially literate, and end up making poor monetary choices. Unfortunately, this contributes to statistics that indicate that, relative to men, women are incredibly under-prepared for, and often impoverished in, their retirement.

- These days, the cost of living is much higher than it once was. This means that your dollars are not going as far as they once did. In 1984, for example, the average cost of a home in Canada was approximately CAD $76,000. If that same house kept up with the rate of inflation, which has hovered just over 3 percent, it would cost approximately CAD $155,000 today. But the reality is that Canada's average home now costs approximately CAD $370,000. When you relate that to average income, in 1984 a home cost a family just under two times their annual income (based on an average inflation-adjusted income of approximately CAD $49,000). Sure, today's average household income has risen to approximately CAD $60,000, but a home now costs just over six times a household's annual income.

  The Canadian Consumer Price Index, as managed and maintained by Statistics Canada, showcases the rise in prices since 1984 of the following goods and services: food, shelter, household operations (including furnishings and equipment), clothing and footwear, transportation (including gasoline), health and personal care, recreation (including education and reading), alcoholic beverages, and energy. The chart below clearly indicates that over the past three decades, the cost of Canadian goods and services has continued to rise. In fact, since 1984, the Consumer Price Index has doubled.[1]

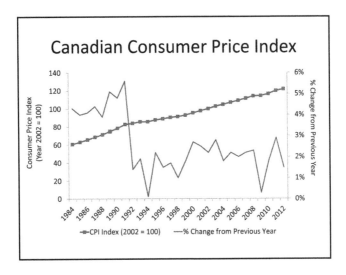

Cost of living statistics for the United States are in line with those for Canada. According to the U.S. Census Bureau, inflation-adjusted income in the United States in 1984 was approximately USD $47,000, and today's average income is just over USD $51,000. In 1984 the average home in the United States sold for approximately USD $97,000, or two times a household's annual income. If that same home from 1984 kept up with inflation, it would cost approximately USD $214,000. But the average home in the United States currently sells for approximately USD $272,000, or five times a household's annual income.[2]

Certainly, in the 1980s mortgage interest rates were exceptionally high, upward of 20 percent, whereas today they are four or five times lower. But so too are savings rates, largely negating the negative impacts of higher mortgage interest rates.

The Consumer Price Index, which is managed and maintained by the U.S. Department of Labor's Bureau of Labor Statistics, indicates a doubling of prices since 1984 — similar to Canadian trends. The chart below showcases the increase in the cost of goods in the United States. Note that in the United States, the Consumer Price Index start-year of 100 is 1984, versus 2002 in Canada, but the chart still conveys the same message — the cost of living is on the rise.[3]

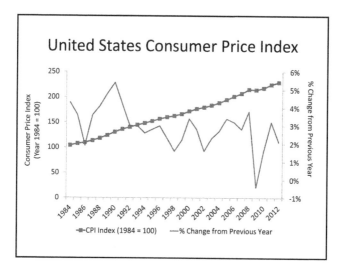

Homes are just one example of the significant increases in the cost of living. Education, cars, and other consumer products cost more today as well. Further to this, because many young women are choosing to delay forming a household with a partner, living expenses to support herself, such as groceries, housing, and travel, are not shared until later in life.

- Many young women are choosing to pursue their education post–high school. The costs of college, university, and trade or technical schools are significantly higher than even a decade ago, resulting in young women taking on high amounts of student debt. In Canada, for example, since 1990 the average tuition and compulsory fees for undergraduates have risen over 6 percent annually — over two-and-a-half times the rate of inflation. According to the National Center for Education Statistics, in the United States, tuition and compulsory fees have risen by over 3.5 percent annually since 1990, which is just slightly above historical inflation rates over the same time period.[4] The investment in education pays off royally over the course of a young woman's career, but shouldering heavy loads of student debt is hard when starting out.

- Since the financial crisis of 2008 and 2009, the quality of jobs and associated benefits, such as pension plans, available to most educated graduates is much lower than in previous decades, which has translated into lower incomes. Ideally, this issue should resolve itself with a stronger economy, but at the present moment underemployment — working at a lower-level job than an individual is qualified for — is rampant.

- If and when a young woman chooses to have a family — raising a family costs hundreds of thousands of dollars — she removes herself from the workforce for a certain period of time. Her income and benefits are often drastically cut back throughout her time off. While she's on leave, her colleagues move ahead, benefiting from their continued efforts in the workplace. Though it's not legally permissible to overlook a woman for job promotions and raises who has taken leave to raise her family, it happens, simply due to the fact she missed valuable working experiences while on parental leave.

- Many young women don't know how to stand up for themselves and their income, so they often make less than their male colleagues. Current stats indicate women earn, on average, 20 percent less than their male colleagues for doing the same job. Sadly, government and corporate policies in North America are draconian and don't adequately prevent this discrimination from persisting. Chapter 5 goes into detail on how to close the income gap.

- The desire to keep up her image as independent, hip, attractive, and intelligent tempts a young woman to overspend on social outings, clothing, shoes, nails, travel, cars, and more. What's behind this are thousands of marketing messages that coax us into spending and use social pressure to further the persuasion. Coupled with the influence of marketing campaigns is easy access to credit. From age 18 on, young women can take out loans, apply for credit cards, and qualify for convenient "do not pay until sometime way in the future" deals.

   Some women characterize their overspending as an addiction. For the shopaholic, the thrill of buying the latest and greatest styles or technology gives her an adrenalin rush that eventually wears off. To keep her pumped-up feeling, she'll buy something else to experience that next rush of excitement. What's so unfortunate about this addiction is that material things can't make a young woman truly happy. They only temporarily fill a void.

As young women, we often bizarrely justify our purchases with the argument that we have jobs and can afford to shop, or the coveted item we just purchased was on sale, or we're young and only live once, or the rest of our bills are paid up. But these justifications are misleading — just because we have jobs or feel we deserve to treat ourselves, doesn't mean we can truly afford our purchases.

Being an indebted shopaholic will hold you back from achieving your financial goals. It's not cool to be in a position where you can't afford to pay off your credit card, or you have to live paycheque to paycheque and can never get ahead. This scenario steals power away from you and makes you vulnerable.

STOP TRYING TO LOOK LIKE A MILLIONAIRE, A MODEL, OR SOMEONE FAMOUS

Imagine what it would be like if young women put as much emphasis on building their net worth — what a woman has left over when her liabilities (what she owes) are subtracted from her assets (what she owns) — as so many do on spending hundreds of dollars on a whim for the latest jeans, or tens of thousands of dollars on a hip new sport utility vehicle. Sound boring? Believe me, it's not. Not only could we afford to have places of our own, take time off between jobs, or tuck away savings for a rainy day, we would still have enough money to enjoy trips, trends, and more in moderation. Having money increases our opportunities to enjoy life and reduces debt-induced stress.

Your net worth is important because it is what will fund the life that you want to create. It will enable you to pay for your wedding, buy a home, send your children to university, purchase a cottage, and travel the world. It will also be your safety net in retirement — which, by the way, is much closer than you think.

Retirement will be more expensive for us than for previous generations because women are living longer and, as previously mentioned, the cost of living is increasing. Growing your net worth will be critical in preparing for your future.

Despite commonly held belief, your net worth has nothing to do with how much money you make. Instead, it's about learning to keep what you've worked so hard to earn. That's right — you could earn $300,000 a year, but if you don't keep it, you're no better off than someone who earns $30,000 a year and doesn't keep it. Sure, higher incomes can afford luxuries like a snazzy car, a larger home, or extravagant trips, but if you don't direct your money toward building your net worth through a combination of debt reduction and asset growth, you'll have nothing left over when your income eventually dries up.

This notion is contrary to our perceptions of wealthy people. Often, we believe it's the people driving the latest high-end vehicles or living in the chic downtown houses who have wealth. But that's not necessarily the case. Many of these individuals do not own their cars and homes outright and are instead working on a cashless system — living paycheque to paycheque, using credit to pay for just about everything, and trying to keep up with monthly payments. Sure, the greater their income, the greater the payments they can afford, but in many cases, their money is spent repaying loans for things that are not considered to be assets, like a vehicle, computer, furniture, or rent. The reality is that most of the people who look wealthy are actually broke!

Still not convinced? Wealthy women don't always look the part. My self-made millionaire aunt, for example, flies in economy class and always asks for a discount when she shops. Having made her fortune owning and growing her business in interior design, she also knows how to spot great deals on furniture, art, jewellery, and clothing. She's not afraid to rummage through second-hand or consignment shops to save money by finding unique treasures for herself or her clients. While so many wannabe-wealthy women drive around in Porsches, my aunt drives a fully paid-for Toyota. Among her top recommendations in the many great pieces of advice she's given me over the years are to live within my means and focus on growing my net worth.

You don't need to become a financial guru or money mongrel, someone who sleeps, eats, and breathes money, as you shift your focus from shopaholic to financially savvy behaviour. Nope. You simply need to adopt the same habits as financially successful women, like my aunt.

Self-made millionaire women repeatedly chalk their success up to following four key financial principles centred on building net worth.

Principle #1: Savvy spending.

Self-made millionaire women spend within their means, and even when they were just starting out, they never borrowed to finance the purchase of non-assets (things that do not grow in value). If a self-made millionaire woman wants to take a trip with her family to Australia, she has cash to pay for it. These women are debt-averse and work on the cash system (described in chapter 2). They've also struck a healthy balance between spending money on the things that make them happy and saving for the future.

Principle #2: Earn more.

Wealthy women find resourceful ways to make more money beyond their regular income. They fight hard for equal pay relative to their male counterparts — this is still a major issue, not only in North America, as noted earlier in this chapter, but in developed countries around the globe. Wealthy women often create small side businesses doing what they are passionate about, or take on additional work that complements their skill sets, like freelance writing.

Principle #3: Save and invest for the future.

Many experts recommend that people save at least 10 percent of everything they earn in order to build a financial safety net for the future. But self-made millionaire women save more; 15–20 percent of everything they make. This is because they've clued in to the fact that these days, the cost of living is ever-increasing, as is the length of our lives, meaning we'll be living longer in a more expensive environment.

Principle #4: Give back.

Successful women have incorporated giving right into their financial plans because they've figured out that the more you give, the more you receive in return. It doesn't matter if you believe in karma or not; the facts show that the benefits of giving your time, talent, and money appear in a variety of forms, including promotions, leadership opportunities, expanded networks, increased sales, and much more. Many wealthy women claim that part of their rise to financial success came through giving even when they were not so wealthy.

By following these principles, a young woman can start to grow her net worth — and *that's* empowering.

KNOWING WHERE YOU ARE AND PLANNING WHERE YOU WANT TO GO

What is your net worth today? Not sure how to tell? If you're a busy person, or if you're using more than one financial product, keeping track of your money can be challenging. Many young women have more than one bank account, investment account, loan, credit card, and ATM card. And when you layer on the fact people often use multiple banks, passwords, and advisers, it's even more confusing. But it's important to keep track of your hard-earned dough so that you can identify where your money is going and whether you're achieving your net-worth goals, and if something flies off the rails, you can take immediate action to rectify the situation.

Experts recommend spending no more than 10 minutes a week monitoring your personal finances. One of the best ways to track your monetary progress is through a net-worth spreadsheet. For those non-technical, non-finance ladies out there, there's no need to get freaked out. Start by marking the date at the top of your spreadsheet. Then, identify all your assets — things you own. Record the name of the institution where each of your accounts is held, followed by the type of account and how much money is in it. To get a handle on how many accounts you have, look at all the statements that come in the mail or, better yet, view your account online and save a tree.

Once you've listed your assets, total them up. For example, you might have an investment account with $5,000 and a savings account with $2,000, for a total of $7,000 in assets.

ASSETS	
Investment Account	$5,000
Savings Account	$2,000
TOTAL	$7,000

Do the same with your liabilities — things you owe money on. Identify where each account is held, the type of liability it is, and how much you owe. So, if you have a car loan with $10,000 owing and a student loan with $15,000 owing, you have a total of $25,000 in liabilities.

LIABILITIES	
Car Loan	$10,000
Student Loan	$15,000
TOTAL	**$25,000**

Once you've listed your assets and liabilities, subtract your liabilities from your assets, and voila — that's your net worth. In this example, your net worth is negative $18,000. You've probably guessed by now that having a negative net worth isn't great because it means that you owe more than you own. But don't fret, *Well-Heeled* is going to show you how to increase your net worth and change that negative into a positive that will keep growing well after you've turned the last page of this book.

NET WORTH	
Assets	$7,000
Liabilities	$25,000
TOTAL	**($18,000)**

Again, over time, and by adopting the habits of wealthy women, you'll grow your net worth through a combination of asset growth and debt reduction. And one of the best ways to begin this process is tracking where you are now and setting realistic net-worth goals for the future. Between now and turning the last page of *Well-Heeled*, start to think about your net worth goal for this year and three or more years down the road.

CHAPTER 2
Frugal Is the New Sexy

FASHIONING FRUGALITY

I purchased my first home when I got my first job out of university at the age of 21. I'd worked very hard to squirrel away money for a small down payment from my part-time and summer jobs throughout my four years of study. It was a huge financial stretch for me, but I knew that, in the long term, buying a place would be an excellent investment. Soon after taking possession, big expenses started to pop up. The screen door needed replacing ($300), the carpets were filthy and required cleaning ($200), the furnace hadn't been serviced in three years ($400), the humidifier broke ($150), and the water heater conked out ($1,500). Sure, I'd had a home inspection and knew I would need to plan for the repair and replacement of certain aspects of my home over the coming years, but these expenses ganged up on me within months of signing my mortgage documents. I'd barely built up any savings in my emergency fund before I'd emptied the account.

What further frustrated me was, as a first-time homebuyer, I had next to nothing in the way of furniture, cleaning supplies,

and basic food staples like flour and spices. So for the first few months, I slept on my mattress on the floor, borrowed cleaning supplies, shopped from my parents' refrigerator, and made do with the clothing I had, even though my work colleagues sported slick suits and the latest patent leather pumps.

When I asked around as to how my peers were able to afford their new cars, couches, clothes, electronics, and more, most responded that they'd charged their purchases to their credit cards or qualified for "do not pay until whenever" programs. I, on the other hand, was, and still am, highly debt averse, and so instead of borrowing to finance purchases for my home, I waited it out.

When I finally felt I could afford to begin purchasing furnishings for my home, I skipped looking at big-box stores and went straight to discount bins, garage sales, eBay, Craigslist, Kijiji, and local second-hand furniture websites. Over the course of a year I sourced out used couches, a desk, a new stove, art, end tables, a dining-room table, a kitchen table, a guest bedroom set, and main bedroom furniture. I paid cash for everything and spent less than $3,500 to furnish my small home.

You may be thinking, Wow, Lesley-Anne's place must have looked awfully shabby! But that was simply not the case. Much of what I purchased was high quality, gently used, or still in its original wrapping, and I took free advice from my interior designer aunt on how to display my pieces of furniture. Over the seven years that I lived in that house, my home was featured in various media publications on four separate occasions as being a "classy and hip" place in Calgary. The angle of each story centred around frugality and what I was able to purchase on a shoestring budget.

When the time came to sell my place in 2012 and move to my second home (a downtown condo), I went right back online, posted my furniture for sale (which didn't match the design of my new home), and sold nearly everything for a whopping $2,500. (As you probably know, furniture rapidly depreciates in value, and to have recovered as much resale value as I did was incredible.)

In those early years of home ownership, I chose to be frugal because I didn't want to take on any additional debt, as my cash flow was very tight to begin with. I learned lifelong skills, like how to negotiate for bargains, use online coupons, shop in discount stores, barter, and trade. Certainly today, at 30 years old, my income is much higher, and I can afford to spend more money on the things I want. But I just can't help my frugal self — I still love a good bargain and hate to throw money out the window.

CHEAPSKATES ARE OUT; FRUGALITY IS EN VOGUE

I'm not a cheapskate, but I sure do enjoy saving money on my purchases where and when I can. Saving money actually drives much of my purchasing behaviour because the more money I can keep, the greater my net worth and the more options I have to do what I want with my life.

Frugal living is different from being a cheapskate. Frugal people maximize the dollars they've worked hard to earn by negotiating prices, finding deals, couponing, buying on sale, and determining the best ways to buy products and services for the lowest possible price. Sure, sometimes my friends think I'm cheap because I drive a second-hand, affordable, fuel-efficient Volkswagen; I love free events; I buy in bulk; and Kijiji is my best friend. But I disagree. I never go without. I'm simply a smart spender, and my bank account proves it.

Cheapskates, on the other hand, have a bad rap for not buying what they need, when they need it, because they are afraid to spend their money. When they do spend, they'll often buy a cheap product that doesn't last, which then creates unnecessary waste and costs more in the long term because it breaks and needs to be replaced. Here are a few examples of the differences between being cheap and being frugal.

CHEAP	FRUGAL
Cheapskates purchase the lowest-priced product regardless of quality.	Frugal young ladies are willing to pay more for affordable quality products.
Cheapskates show up at dinner parties empty-handed.	Frugal young ladies host potluck dinners so that nobody has to shoulder the entire grocery bill.
Cheapskates avoid tipping a service provider at all costs.	Frugal young ladies tip according to the quality of service.
When the bill comes, cheapskates bolt out of the restaurant and hope their friends overpaid.	Frugal young ladies divide up the dinner bill according to who ate what.
Cheapskates pirate books, movies, and music.	Frugal young ladies borrow or swap books, movies, and music from friends or the library.
Cheapskates never offer to pay for a pal's coffee.	Frugal young ladies swap back and forth between who pays for coffee.
Cheapskates will forgo spending money on essential items like medication, transit passes, and baby formula.	Frugal young ladies won't skimp on items that support their health and livelihood, but they will find the best deal on those products and apply for financial assistance or tax credits to afford them.

The unfortunate reality is that, despite their belief that they're saving money, cheapskates often end up broke because they buy low-quality things and do not know how to spot good value. Frugal young ladies do not spend frivolously. They take time to research their purchases and know what is and is not a good deal.

Regardless of whether you're an overspender or a cheapskate, with just a little effort, you can live frugally and save money without compromising your lifestyle. Remember from chapter 1 that research shows wealthy women live within their means and frugally. Dr. Thomas Stanley has conducted extensive studies on thousands of wealthy men and women. In his book *Stop Acting Rich ... And Start Living Like a Real Millionaire*, he discusses how most millionaires keep meticulous budgets, live in homes valued at less than $300,000, and purchase rather than lease their cars (and those cars are often second-hand). And surprisingly, typical millionaire women never pay more than $140 for a pair of shoes — and you know as well as I do that Jimmy Choos don't fall into that price bracket!

JOIN THE FRUGAL MOVEMENT

Being broke is frustrating, embarrassing, and definitely not sexy. It limits your options. Imagine what you could do if, instead of owing $20,000, you had $20,000. You could go back to school, take a trip, save for retirement, pay for your wedding. Whereas if you owe $20,000, you either pay it back or you don't — and if you don't, the bank will come and repossess your car, your television, and your Manolo Blahniks ... okay, maybe not your Manolo Blahniks, but certainly everything else that has resale value.

If you're busting your budget each month, you have three options: borrow money, increase your income, or reduce your spending. Borrowing money is a bad idea because it just deals with the symptoms rather than the actual problem, which is overspending. Increasing your income takes time and can be helpful, but overspenders typically end up spending this extra income. Reducing your spending and learning to live frugally gets to the root of the overspending problem.

Recently, as a result of a slower economy and serious household-budget limitations, frugal living has gained major momentum, as evidenced by hyped-up online couponing and bloggers chatting up their readers about the latest deals. There isn't a day goes by that I don't watch a program or read a newspaper and learn about how North Americans are finding creative ways to stash their cash.

If you want to watch your net worth grow, join the frugal movement. You won't have to sacrifice basic needs, social interaction, or even your image. In fact, women who spend within their means report that they have all the material things they need, less stress, and more rich and fulfilling personal relationships relative to their indebted peers.

Are you ready to save money?

FRUGAL FUNDAMENTALS

There are three elements to frugal living: the cash system, savvy spending, and resourcefulness. Transitioning from credit to the cash system helps curb overspending and promotes living within one's means. Savvy spending means saving money on your purchases, while being resourceful means finding more money or stretching out your dollars.

When the cash system, savvy spending, and resourcefulness are combined, frugality saves money and reduces waste. But underneath it all, the golden rule of frugality is this: a great deal on something that you can't afford or don't need is never a great deal!

THE CASH SYSTEM

Breaking overspending habits is difficult, as they've been established over many years. A young woman may have even watched her parents struggle with overspending and learned bad habits from their behaviours. Fortunately, there is an effective way to break the cycle of overspending and being broke. It begins with a form of delayed gratification: saving up for small purchases, and paying for these items in cash.

The day I bought my first designer handbag is a classic example of the power of delayed gratification. It was 2007, and I was shopping on Black Friday at the flagship Nordstrom store in Seattle, when I saw a beautiful purse with soft black leather, a gold-studded opening, and buckle clasps that snapped shut with the flick of a finger. The handbag even smelled rich and lovely — the neighbouring perfume counter might have had something to do with it, but I didn't care. It was love at first sight, touch, and smell.

When I reached inside to check the price, I was overjoyed to learn that the purse had been marked down 50 percent. As I handed over my $150 in cash, which was a lot of money for me at 23 years old, I was filled with excitement.

Under normal circumstances, out of sheer monetary guilt, I would have never entertained such a purchase. But this was a special occasion; for the first time in two years, I had positive cash flow.

As I mentioned at the beginning of this chapter, when I was 21 years old, I'd stretched to purchase my first home, which buried me financially in unexpected expenses and unpleasant surprises. My house wound up being an excellent long-term investment, but in those early years of home ownership, I had a classic case of home poverty, where I could barely afford anything but my house.

To make ends meet, I'd rented out my spare room, taken on additional work as a freelance writer, and couponed for absolutely everything I bought. Each month I got closer to getting out of the red, and as a reward for achieving positive cash flow, I promised to buy myself a designer handbag.

Purchasing that bag represented more than just fine stitching and a sassy design. It was a symbol that I could afford to pay for it in cash and that I was capable of transforming a rotten financial situation into a liberating experience. Buying that bag with money that I'd saved, rather than borrowed, was powerful. What I didn't realize then, but do now, is that those years of living lean, resurfacing from the red, and rewarding myself with a handbag shifted my mentality on spending; I finally understood the power of spending within my means ... just like wealthy women do.

Have you ever wondered why some people carry a lot of cash in their wallets or only pay for purchases with debit cards rather than credit cards? Many of these individuals work on the cash system as a way of curbing their shopaholic tendencies and spending within their means. Rather than charging purchases to their Visa, Amex, or MasterCard, these individuals formulate an idea of how much money they plan on spending in any particular week, withdraw that amount of cash, and when the money runs out, so too does their spending. In the case of using a debit card, these individuals keep all their receipts, and once they've reached their spending limit for the week, they leave their debit card at home and stop spending.

A by-product of spending on a cash system is that these folks become frugal, which means they are keen to stretch their dollars as far as possible by reducing unnecessary spending and taking advantage of discounts, sales, and coupons.

Many young shopaholic women who are in too deep work on a cashless system. This means they are using their credit card or line of credit to carry them to the next paycheque. When they get their next paycheque, they pay off some, or all, of the debt they accrued the previous two weeks, and rack up the debt again over the next two weeks. This is a cashless system whereby a young woman has no cash to carry her through to the next pay period. She is effectively running in circles and never getting ahead financially.

Does this sound somewhat familiar? Ladies, if you want to break free from broke, you cannot carry on spending as usual. You need to move to a cash system.

Take your credit cards out of your purse and cancel all but one. Despite what marketers will tell you, no one needs more than one credit card. Keep the credit card with the longest and best credit history. This remaining credit card is solely for emergencies and needs to be stored in a place where you can't easily access it. That might mean throwing it in a Ziploc baggie, filling the baggie with water, and putting it in the freezer. Or storing it in a safety deposit box at your local bank. Whatever you choose to do, you need to get it out of your sight, to reduce the temptation to use it.

The only card you should keep in your purse is your debit card, and it cannot be connected to your line of credit or savings account. If it is, go to your bank and have them disconnect it. Your debit card should only allow you access to withdraw and deposit money to your chequing account — the account your paycheques are deposited into and your bills are paid from.

Next, go to your bank's online banking website and set up automatic online bill payments for your monthly bills, like cable and electricity, so that they are paid directly from your bank account and are NOT charged to your credit card. If you've been charging them to your credit card, phone the utility provider and stop the charges. Your mortgage or rent, car payment, loan payments, and insurance should also be paid directly, and automatically, from your bank account, not from any other source of credit.

Once you're set to pay your bills directly from your bank account, you need to take a moment to calculate the amount of money you require for purchases until you receive your next paycheque, which is typically two weeks away. These expenses might be things like groceries, coffees, gifts, meals out, fuel for your vehicle, home maintenance items, computer supplies, recreational fees, clothes, books, et cetera.

Let's say these expenses total $400 for the two weeks until your next paycheque. You'll need to go to the ATM and pull out that amount of money in cash. You'll use this cash to pay for your expenses, and when you run out of cash, you're out — no more spending. As an alternative, you can pay for these expenses with your debit card, but you'll need to keep a running total of what you're spending by adding up your receipts, and when you've reached the end of your budget, you need to stop spending.

I generally recommend that if you really struggle with overspending, hide your debit card along with your credit card. You can withdraw your cash from a bank teller, thus completely eliminating the need to have your debit card in your wallet. Using physical cash is better than using a debit card because a debit card still allows you access to more cash beyond your spending limit.

Transitioning to the cash system can be a huge challenge for young women when their entire paycheques are gobbled up with debt and bill payments. If your budget is totally maxed out, ease your way into the cash system over the course of three or four paycheques. Making the transition to the cash system will also mean you'll need to cut out unnecessary spending so that you can pay for essential things with cash.

Once on the cash system, you will naturally become more conscious of how you are spending your money and will want to adopt the principles of frugal living. For example, if you have $100 for both groceries and a book purchase, but you spend it all on dinners out instead, you won't have any more money to buy the groceries and the book. Under normal circumstances this is when a young woman would pull out her credit card, but that is no longer an option.

Oftentimes, it helps to pair up with a friend and make the transition to the cash system together. By setting weekly spending goals and discussing your spending challenges, you can hold each other accountable throughout the process.

If you are a credit card point–collecting enthusiast, you can still operate on the cash system by charging a purchase to your credit card and paying it off in full from your bank account a few hours later. Some banks will even allow you to set up automatic repayments to your credit card each day so that what you spend during the day is paid off in full that evening. But — and this is a huge, huge but — this only works if you are highly disciplined and have the cash to pay off the charges. If you go to sleep at night without fully paying off your purchases, you need to shift to the traditional cash system because your current approach isn't working. No amount of points is ever worth going into debt for.

Moving to a cash system is the first step toward breaking the cycle of overspending, and living within your means. This, in turn, stops the further accumulation of debt. Once you're using the cash system, you can then isolate your debts and create a plan to dig your way out from underneath debt's nasty cloche. This is when you will start to see your net worth grow — and that's an awesome reward.

There is yet another reason to carry cash: in case of an emergency. For some strange reason, of which I don't think a social experiment is necessary to prove because we live in an electronic society, most young women don't carry much cash in their wallets at the best of times. I used to be one of those young women using my debit card for just about everything, but I started carrying cash a few years ago after my car died on the highway when I was en route home from a speaking engagement I'd had in Banff, Alberta. When I reached the mechanic's shop back in Banff — tow truck and all — the Interac and credit card machines were down, and I couldn't pay for my tow or my repairs. I had to hitch yet another ride to get to my bank to withdraw money.

That experience made me feel extremely vulnerable because I was essentially dependent upon the kindness of strangers. Sure, it turned out fine, and fortunately I was unscathed, but it got me thinking about emergencies in general. In the case of an emergency or natural disaster, ABM machines could go down, be out of geographic range, or be otherwise inaccessible for a variety of reasons. If a young woman has no cash, she may have to forgo essential purchases like food, hotel rooms, or fuel. Having no cash at all makes a young woman vulnerable. I now try to carry at least $100 in my wallet and keep a few hundred dollars in cash at home at all times.

SAVVY SPENDING

Get Ruthless

Get ruthless about your financial priorities. What's more important, sporting new Lululemon gear at the gym you rarely go to, or saving up a down payment so you can buy your own place? If you care about your net worth, you should wear your existing workout gear, cancel your expensive gym membership, sign up for a less expensive outdoor fitness boot camp, and start a savings program for your down payment.

To help prioritize your spending, adopt the following rule: if you don't need it, don't buy it — no matter how good the sale is. Certainly, there are exceptions to this rule, like if you've specifically set aside funds to reward yourself for achieving a particular goal, but in general, it's a safe and frugal rule to live by.

Sometimes it's difficult to discern whether a purchase falls into the needs or the wants category. If you're having difficulty prioritizing between the two, it often helps to consult with a frugal friend who's holding you accountable for your overspending, and/or to wait 48 hours before making a purchase, which gives you some breathing room to think about your financial priorities and often reduces the temptation to spend on unnecessary things.

Get Protection

Your money is too darn important not to protect, so be practical. Frugal women don't leave money or other things of value like phones, passwords, purses, passports, car keys, or jewellery lying around, and you shouldn't either. Wealthy women also adopt tried-and-true anti-fraud best practices like changing passwords regularly and only using secure Internet sources. Chapter 8 goes into further detail on effective anti-fraud techniques.

Pare Down

If you're ready to buy something, pare down your purchase, like selecting a two-dollar regular coffee versus a five-dollar whipped mocha Frappuccino.

Do you really need all the bells and whistles on your new car, like a sunroof and GPS? Could you get by with less, save thousands, and achieve the same result by opening your windows and pulling up a map on your iPhone? Better yet, could you ignore the persuasive new-car salesman for a few days and find that same car second-hand?

Or, if you're thinking of signing up for online dating, take advantage of a free trial subscription before handing over $30 per month for a service you have yet to try. If you're pleased with the results and decide to go ahead with the service, evaluate the variety of subscriptions and whether you can get by with the bare minimum.

When purchasing or renting a home, consider a smaller and more affordable place. Besides lower monthly payments, there will be less space to furnish, heat, and provide other utilities for. Then review your cable, Internet, phone, and cellular plans. If you use a landline only once in a while, get rid of it and direct people to your cell phone instead. Consider bundling your utility services and reducing the number of cable channels you receive; most shows can be viewed or purchased online on an as-needed basis, anyway.

Whatever you're in the market for, always review your alternatives and consider a smaller, less expensive purchase rather than the full package.

Negotiate

In the words of my late grandfather, "If you don't ask, you don't get," and so I negotiate for everything. When I'm buying furniture, shopping for clothes, or paying for a professional development course, I always ask for a better price. Rarely have I been turned down. In fact, I would say that 90 percent of the time, the person I'm dealing with is eager to keep my business, and so they work with me on a better price, or sweeten the deal by offering me more value for my money.

Everything is negotiable. Bigger-ticket items like houses, cars, and furniture often have significant price flexibility simply because they cost more than average purchases. But less expensive products like clothing or electronics also have wiggle room on price. When you ask to negotiate on price, it often helps to offer to pay cash (so the merchant doesn't get charged a fee to process your transaction), present a competitive offer, and be prepared to take your business elsewhere.

You can even negotiate the interest rates on your loans, mortgage, and credit cards (more on this in chapter 4). A 10-minute phone call with a customer service manager is all it takes to reduce your rate and save thousands of dollars.

Bargain Hunt

You can save hundreds of dollars each month by bargain hunting. For regular purchases like groceries or cleaning supplies, buy in bulk and use coupons. These days, many stores offer downloadable coupons online.

The best time to shop is when there are sales, so sign up for email notifications and watch for red or yellow clearance signs. For example, I wait until the first Tuesday of each month to do my massive grocery shopping because I get a 10-percent discount and double my loyalty points. If what you want isn't marked down, ask for a discount and offer to pay with cash. Always check for rebates and subsidies.

Whatever you do, don't be a cheapskate. Avoid products that have a reputation for shoddy workmanship — they'll break and likely cost you more in the long run.

Make Eco-Friendly Choices

Despite what you may think, being environmentally conscious can save you money — and you don't have to purchase expensive solar panels, sacrifice daily showers, or live "off the grid." If your home has a yard, or you have access to a community garden, you can grow your own food. When purchasing groceries, save yourself a few dollars by taking your own fabric bags and walking to and from the store. If you're used to driving, try using public transit, carpooling, walking, running, cycling, or in-line skating instead. In the summer of 2013, I purchased a bicycle that was on sale, and I didn't drive my vehicle for over seven weeks. This may have had something to do with why my car didn't start right away the next time, so I probably won't let it sit for as long next year — but I saved over $300 in fuel that summer.

Save on utility bills by washing laundry in cold water and installing reduced-flow shower heads. You may even want to scale back the length of your showers; set the timer on your smartphone to 7 minutes rather than your usual 15 minutes. On cold days put on a sweater and turn the temperature down a few degrees. On hot days strip down and reduce the air conditioning in your house. Turn out the lights and properly seal your doors and windows. Keeping your vehicle well maintained will also reduce pollution and extend its life.

Buy Used

As I mentioned earlier in this chapter, I have no qualms about purchasing things that are of high quality and have been gently used. In fact, besides the thrill I get from saving mega dough, I feel pretty good that what I'm buying isn't headed to the landfill. My favourite sources are Kijiji, eBay, Craigslist, garage sales, and going-out-of-business sales.

Just to give you an idea of how much some of my furniture cost for my first home, I scored my stove for $60, dining-room table for $50, TV stand for $8, coffee and end tables for $75, master bedroom bed set and mattress for $500, guest room bed set for $300, and couches for $500. Some of my furniture was even free! Most of the items were barely used, and some were still in their original wrapping.

My model-year 2007 Dell computer died in 2012; it had served me well, through the writing of two books and MBA school, but it was actually wheezing and hissing ... always a bad sign. So I purchased my MacBook Pro and large LCD screen from a friend who was hocking the pair on Kijiji for $1,500. Seeing as my pal buys a new computer every six months (which is so incredibly un-frugal), I scored a barely used, top-of-the-line computer, with software and the matching LCD screen, saving more than $1,000. He even threw in a few small accessories for free.

Before buying something new, check out whether you can find a gently used version.

Get Rid of "Stuff"

When I sold my 1,500-square-foot home in 2012 and moved into a 900-square-foot condo that same year, I learned two huge lessons about the accumulation of "stuff." First, the less you have, the more you'll save. Second, if you don't need something any longer, rid yourself of it right away. What good is it to store a desk in your garage for five years if it's only going to collect dust? Sell it!

Rather than tossing my excess furniture, sporting equipment, and appliances in the trash, I turned to Kijiji to sell it to local buyers. Using my iPad and cell phone camera, I created compelling ads for free. Once buyers were in my house, many bought more items than what they had originally come for. The buyers paid cash and moved the pieces out themselves. Within one week, 75 percent of my "stuff" was sold. I chalk the quick sales up to pricing the pieces competitively and taking nice photos.

I certainly didn't make a profit on anything I sold, but I recovered a fair chunk of change, which I put toward moving expenses and closing costs on my new place.

My second downsizing strategy was to donate the remainder of my "stuff" to local charities. For bigger items, the charities picked up the goods right from my front door. For smaller pieces, I dropped them off.

Even today I'll sell things I don't need any longer online. When I'm keen to get rid of shoes, clothing, or purses, I will swap with my friends or donate the items to the local women's shelter. Rarely do I ever throw something in the trash.

Avoiding the accumulation of "stuff" is always your most frugal option. Second to that, save money and reduce waste by buying and selling used goods.

Get Healthy

Being active and eating healthy will save you money and reduce your waistline. If you smoke or drink too much, cut it out. Rather than going out to a movie with your friends, strap on your Rollerblades, hop on your bicycle, snap on your cross-country skis, or go for a walk. You can catch up with your pals or even go on a date while burning calories.

Weather permitting, my friends and I plan our get-togethers around being active, even if it's just walking to get a coffee or biking to an outdoor music festival. Certainly, we eat at restaurants from time to time in celebration of someone's birthday or big accomplishment, but often we'll trade in the fancy linen napkins to play Frisbee and barbecue at someone's home.

You can also save boatloads of money and manage your daily calorie count by eating at home and reducing visits to your local café. Late in the summer of 2013, I had reconstructive surgery to fix my broken jaw (more on this in chapter 8). For nearly 12 weeks, I was on a blended diet of homemade soups and smoothies. My dietary limitations, combined with the fact I couldn't talk well, as my mouth was wired shut, kept me away from lunch and coffee meetings. Due to the nature of my business, which involves a lot of meetings at restaurants, I was shocked by how much money I saved over three months — a whopping $1,000. This was a reminder of how much little things like lattes and mango salads can add up.

Entertain Yourself on the Cheap

Rather than buying tickets to the hottest show in town, watch it on YouTube with your friends over a glass of wine. And forget about ordering in food; try out a new recipe at home. Sign up for free programs to learn a new language, sport, dance, or other art form. If you have a family, entertain them with inexpensive and locally sponsored shows and festivals. Swap books, CDs, and movies with friends, or borrow them for free from your local library. Volunteer your time to help a senior, improve the local women's shelter, or participate in a neighbourhood cleanup — you'll probably make some high-quality friends in the process.

Forget about planning expensive dates with your love interest, and spend romantic time chit-chatting or getting active.

Do More Yourself

Google is amazing. Last year I was minutes away from hopping in my car and driving over to my local electronics store to purchase a new printer. The wireless function had conked out on my HP Officejet when I'd reset my network — but instead of forking over $200 for the latest laser jet, I found how to solve my problem on Google.

There are so many things you can do yourself that you would ordinarily pay someone else to do, such as car maintenance, house cleaning, painting, cooking, and repairing. Before you call your handy-dandy plumber, go online and see if you can find a way to unplug your sink yourself.

You may even have a friend who's a fix-it expert and would be willing to swap services. Last year, for example, I swapped expertise with my buddy Ryan, who is a pipefitter. He hooked up my barbeque to my new gasline (I didn't have the right tools), and I helped him with his passport application.

Watch for the Perils of Small Purchases

Consider this: 25-year-old Marda goes out for lunch twice a week, totalling $20; buys a regular coffee once a day, totalling $15 a week; meets her gal pals for wine on Fridays for $20; and goes for dinner on Saturdays with her significant other for $20. Her small weekly expenditures total $75 a week.

Let's also say that Marda carries on spending $75 a week on small food-and-beverage purchases throughout her working career, from age 25 to 65 (40 years in total). If you total up her purchases annually and compound them at the rate of inflation, 3.5 percent, throughout her working career, she will have spent approximately $335,000.

Wowie!!!! Marda will have literally ingested the equivalent of a house purchase — not to mention that many of the foods and drinks she will purchase, rather than make at home, contain unhealthy ingredients! Just imagine how awesome it would be for Marda's net worth if she simply cut back on half of these purchases and directed those savings into her retirement plan or paying off her mortgage faster.

I am by no means suggesting that young women, like you or me, stop eating out and enjoying a beverage or two from time to time. Nope. Marda's spending is just an example to draw your attention to the fact that seemingly "small" purchases, whether food or lotto tickets or clothing, can add up to be something quite substantial in the long term.

Reduce the Temptation

If you struggle with temptations to spend, get rid of excess credit. You only need one credit card, so cut up the rest! If you have loads of credit available to spend through your line of credit or credit card, reduce the borrowing limit.

RESOURCEFULNESS

Finding Money

In my early 20s, I made a point of dumping out my change at the end of each day into my piggy bank — yes, I still have a pink piggy bank even today. My change came from purchases, bottle returns, and what I found on the ground and in coat pockets and couch cushions.

At the end of each year, the pig was full, and I would spend over an hour rolling up my change — a dreadfully boring and filthy task. On average I rolled up $250 each year, and it got me thinking about two things. First, small change can really add up (I guess scooping quarters off the ground does pay off). And second, why the heck didn't I just use my change throughout my weeks, rather than collecting it, and put it toward better uses, like purchasing groceries, contributing to my savings account, buying my library membership, or paying to hit balls at the nearby driving range?

So today, I still return bottles, pick up change off the ground, and check my pockets and the nooks and crannies of my purses for money. My piggy bank is empty because all my nickels, dimes, and quarters go toward useful things throughout my weeks. Essentially, I don't let my change waste away in a drawer or my piggy bank, and neither should you!

Money is money, no matter the form, so find it and put it to good use, like repaying your debts or starting a savings program. Check your jacket pockets, purses, penny jars, in between cushions of your couch, and in junk drawers for coins or bills. Once you've moved to the cash system, you'll have even more change kicking around (unless you choose the debit card route).

Use Up What You Have

If you're like me, you probably have 4 different rolls of wrapping paper, 10 rolls of tape, 18 greeting cards, and a few toys and games still in their wrapping stashed in a closet somewhere. Before I run to my local gift shop to buy something new, I always check my stash of goodies to see if I can use what I have. The same goes for groceries. I love to bake, for example, and I tend to have all the supplies to make chocolate cakes, cookies, pies, and more. So, before I rush to my neighbourhood supermarket for ingredients, I cross-reference what I have with what the recipe calls for.

Do you have partially used gift cards that are taking up space in your wallet? Could you put them toward essential purchases like vitamins or fuel? Have you cashed in your pre-purchased online coupons, like those offered by Groupon? If you've got five Starbucks gift cards, save money and use them up!

Re-Gifting and Couponing

In the past, re-gifting, couponing, and bulk-purchase presents were considered social faux pas because they meant the gift-giver was being cheap.

I couldn't disagree more!

Resourceful re-gifting, couponing, and bulk-buying are not the same as being cheap. Besides, stretching your dollars and taking advantage of opportunities to save money will keep you out of debt, reduce waste, and still allow you to spoil everyone on your gift list.

Wrap up that extra garlic press you received for your birthday, and give it to your brother. Otherwise, it'll sit in your cupboard collecting dust!

According to CouponCabin.com, nearly 40 percent of North Americans re-gift presents, and a large majority use coupons when holiday shopping. The most commonly re-gifted items are gift cards and duplicate and unwanted products, but there are some parameters for socially acceptable re-gifting that you should follow.

Ensure the present is in its original wrapping, and don't re-gift something that has clearly been used. Remove your name from any tags or cards, and don't give the gift back to the same person who gifted it to you. Avoid re-gifting intimate or personal hygiene products like underwear, nail clippers, or razors. If you've received a sentimental gift, don't re-gift it, because that could upset the person who gave it to you.

If you've bought something on sale or with a coupon, remove the bright red sale sticker and price tag. While the recipient is opening your gift, don't blurt out how proud you are that you used a coupon; be discreet.

Especially when planning your holiday spending, bulk-buying some items, like stocking stuffers or appreciation gifts for friends or colleagues, is wise. Cash in unused loyalty rewards points or gift cards toward gifts. If you use a gift card to buy another gift card, make sure you pick a round number like $50 rather than re-gifting your card with $42.68 left on it.

If your budget is super tight, don't buy any gifts at all. Make handmade cards, art, and baked goods. Homemade presents are affordable and have loads of sentimental value.

The Barter System

Bartering isn't outdated. The exchange of goods and services rather than paying cash for things you need is a concept alive and well today.

Do you have a special skill set, or do you own something that someone else wants? Trade it for something that you need.

Let's say, for example, that if you want to progress up the leadership ladder at work, you need to learn a new language. You could swap language-tutoring services with your neighbour who teaches second languages in exchange for taking care of his or her children once a week. This would be a cashless transaction, and provide a mutual benefit to both parties.

If You're Going to Spend, At Least Get Something for Free

The average North American consumer carries approximately six different loyalty cards in the hopes of saving money or getting free stuff. Because I love free things and saving money, I'm well above the average. My wallet contains 10 different loyalty cards, and I have two additional key-ring tags attached to my key chain.

The purpose of a loyalty program is to persuade you to change your buying behaviour by consuming more than you would in the absence of a program, and ideally from the same vendor. It's tempting to turn ordinary purchases of groceries, fuel, or shoes into something of value, like free hotels and flights. However, these programs can be complex and may trick even a savvy buyer into overspending. Everyone loves free rewards, but not at the expense of your financial plan.

It makes sense to join a loyalty program only if you're already a loyal shopper; then, it's meaningful and you earn rewards for purchases you'd have made anyway. For most North Americans, this means accumulating credit card or airline points. But there are other programs. If you're a coffee buyer, collect stamps so that your tenth coffee is free. Join the discount club at the grocery store or a bulk-buying-warehouse membership program.

I recommend avoiding rewards programs you don't plan to redeem within a short time frame (two years or less). This is because the longer you wait, the more likely it is the point system will change and adjust to the increasing cost of providing the rewards. Because rewards programs are a privilege and not a right, providers commonly change the rules at the expense of consumers' rewards. If you don't keep up with purchases or payments, your points can disappear. In 2012 the points I needed to redeem for short-haul air travel increased 25 percent. My points became less powerful over time, which put a new spin on the phrase "use it or lose it."

So, maximize the value of your loyalty programs. Depending on the rewards system, you could exchange your points for cash, gifts, contributions to your retirement savings program, electronics, or travel. Keep in mind that redeeming "free" points can also result in your having to pay taxes, surcharges, and fees.

A July 2009 study from the University of Toronto and an economist at the Federal Reserve Bank of Kansas City, found that people would accrue less credit card debt if card companies were barred from offering rewards based on the value of purchases.[1] It's foolish to spend an unplanned $1,000 just to collect points that, when layered with another $25,000 in point-building purchases, can be converted into golf clubs 12 years down the road. If you catch yourself justifying your purchase as a "good deal" because of the loyalty program, reconsider that purchase.

Rewards shouldn't drive your purchase decisions; good financial planning should. Have only one or two credit cards and avoid carrying a balance (you earn points only for new purchases, not for carrying a balance). Before you buy, ask yourself if you can afford the purchase and if the purchase helps build your net worth (buy assets and avoid debt). If it doesn't build your net worth, think again.

FRUGAL DATING

A rotten economy has made extravagant dating nearly impossible. Forget full-priced tickets to Paul McCartney or a romantic helicopter ride. I double-dare you to use a coupon on your next date.

According to CouponCabin's 2011 survey, nearly 20 percent of adults have used a coupon on a first date and received a positive reaction. Of the remaining respondents, 75 percent said they wouldn't be offended if their date used a coupon to pay.

Before you whip out a coupon, gauge whether your date would be cool with it or not. If you think your date is into couponing, crack a joke about your Groupon deal of the day, present the coupon to the server, and carry on with your conversation. If you think your date might freak out, sneak the coupon to the server en route to the washroom.

Times have changed, and it's no longer frowned upon to be frugal while dating. In fact, if frugality is one of your core values, saving money while dating is a great way to test whether your partner is financially compatible with you. There are plenty of inexpensive and creative dating activities that won't cramp your style or your wallet.

Date online. You can join online dating communities like eHarmony or Match and use coupons for your membership. Plus, you can pre-screen your date so that you don't waste time and money getting to know someone who's incompatible with you.

Meet your date at a local coffee house and kick back for a few hours in a casual atmosphere (less than $10). Or, grab coffee to-go and walk around the neighbourhood. Share stories and enjoy the chit-chat.

Get active and walk, run, bike, rollerblade, work out, or toboggan. Head to a park, go for a swim, or spice up a game of tennis with competition — the loser buys the next glass of vino (less than $20). Take advantage of free outdoor festivals and plays.

Rent old movies, or see a flick in the cheap theatres (less than $20). Get to know each other's friends by hosting games night — charades, board games, and appetizers (less than $30). Check out art exhibit openings, book launches, or music releases. Tickets are often free or priced relatively inexpensively (less than $40).

Skip restaurants and turn a weekly grocery trip into a farmer's market adventure. Pick up fresh ingredients for a home-cooked meal, which you can make together. Cooking is romantic, fun, and easy; download free recipes from the Internet and follow along. Enjoy a reasonably priced bottle of wine. If the weather is decent, take your meal outside, light candles, and bundle up in blankets (less than $50).

If you're set on going to a restaurant, find a hole-in-the-wall that's been recommended by someone you trust. Smaller restaurants can be more authentic, intimate, and budget-friendly, and can have higher-quality food than bigger, more popular "hot spots" (less than $100).

Saving money is sexy. Going into debt to impress a date is not. Dating on a budget often inspires creativity and allows you to showcase your true colours. Always remember, the point of a date is to spend time with someone special, not bust your budget.

REWARDING YOURSELF

Frugal living doesn't mean you can't reward yourself from time to time. In fact, it's important to celebrate your income-earning ability, so long as it doesn't get in the way of your long-term financial goals. I like to reward myself when I achieve a particular milestone, such as completing the manuscript for my new book or achieving a certain level of net worth. The key with rewarding yourself is to ensure you can afford it, and when it's linked to a particular accomplishment, it will mean far more than simply splurging on new rock-climbing gear "just because."

CHAPTER 3
So You're on a B@#$%& (Budget)

THAT B@#$%& CAN SAVE YOUR FINANCIAL HEINIE

Jewel was six years out of college and 29 years old when she realized her finances were getting worse, not better. She'd been working as a nurse's aide since graduation, steadily earning raises, but her monthly expenses and debts seemed to be growing rather than shrinking. She'd graduated with about $20,000 in student debt and diligently made payments toward it, but between monthly car, entertainment, furniture, and mortgage payments (she'd qualified for a zero-down mortgage years earlier, when lending rules were very lax), she couldn't figure out where her money seemed to go each month. When her paycheques were deposited on the first and fifteenth of each month, they'd be gone within days.

To track down where her hard-earned money was going, Jewel downloaded a free budget-tracking tool from her bank's online resources. She took an evening out of her busy social schedule to list her income and categorize her expenses. Jewel quickly realized she was running in the red; her expenses were greater than her monthly income.

The simple act of identifying where her money was coming from and going to allowed Jewel to carefully examine where she might cut back in order to start improving her bottom line. For example, she had been spending $100 a month on her cell phone plan and $75 a month on her hair and nails. She called her cell phone provider and signed up for a different plan that still met her needs but cost only $70 a month. She shopped around for a new stylist and aesthetician and found a great alternative for $60 a month. She thought about her grocery shopping and figured she could become a member at the local discount grocer, saving her an additional $30 per month if she shopped in bulk and at non-peak times throughout the month. Then she consolidated her two credit card balances into one at a lower rate, cut up the second card, and calculated an additional $50 a month in savings.

Energized by the fact that she was finding a variety of ways to save money, Jewel prepared her very first forward-looking budget, in which she planned out her spending for the next six months. She used her budget to help guide her spending and find opportunities for further saving. When the temptation to spend beyond her budget arose, she'd curb the temptation by reminding herself of how she'd already planned for fun within her budget: dinners with friends, trips, movies, parties, gifts, and more.

Within a few short months, Jewel started to see her financial situation improve, and she no longer needed overdraft protection for her chequing account. After each month she had $125 left over, so she decided to take half of it and make an extra payment toward her highest-interest debt (her one remaining credit card). She allocated the other half toward a retirement savings plan.

THE BIG BAD *B*-WORD

The word *budget* has earned a bad rap for being old-school, restrictive, and boring, a tool that our grandmothers used to help manage the family finances when credit cards weren't yet a reality. But regardless of whether you like the word or not, budgets are important because they help guide a young woman as she plans her spending and saving. In Dr. Thomas Stanley's books on millionaires, one thing most millionaires had in common, and claimed was key to their financial success, was keeping and maintaining a meticulous budget — a habit they continued even when they'd reached millionaire status.

If the word *budget* irritates you as much as it irritates me, you may want to refer to it in modern-woman terms as "Managing the Bank of Me" (replace *me* with your name).

Managing the Bank of Me involves creating a personal spending plan (i.e., a budget) that allows you to track your dough and work toward living within your means. Don't freak out — creating a personal spending plan is easy, and you don't need to be a spreadsheet genius to figure it out. Simply list your sources of income and your expenses. When you subtract your total expenses from your total income, that's how much money you have left over — your bottom line.

Most people like to create a monthly personal spending plan, while others prefer to prepare a weekly or annual one. I recommend setting up a personal spending plan that is aligned with the frequency of when you get paid; for most people this is biweekly or monthly. Later in the chapter, I'll lay out an example of a personal spending plan that you can follow, but first, let's get organized.

TRACK IT OR LOSE IT

Organization is the cornerstone of building a healthy financial future. If you're financially disorganized, I can guarantee that you will not be able to achieve your financial goals, let alone your personal and professional ones. Studies consistently show that people who are highly organized, set clear goals, *and* write them down are far more likely to achieve them compared to those who have no goals, or even those whose goals are unwritten.

To successfully manage your finances and build your net worth, you need to become financially organized. I'm not talking about having a spreadsheet that lays out every detail of your 10-year personal spending plan; no, I'm talking about knowing and controlling what goes into and out of your bank account each month (a.k.a. budgeting), knowing what your net worth is, and being clear about your financial goals for the future.

If you've got unopened bills, pay stubs, and financial papers strewn across your kitchen table, stuffed in a drawer, or busting out of the glove compartment of your car, it's high time you became financially organized.

It all starts with tracking where your money is coming from, and how much is coming in, by listing your sources of income. Once you know your sources of income, track where your money is going. Open up your online banking and click on your primary account, typically your chequing account. Then open up your credit card account. This is where your transactions are listed. If you don't have online banking, grab your latest account statements, which are typically delivered by snail mail. If you've lost those, call your bank and credit card company, and either sign up for online banking or have your old statements mailed to you (there will probably be a fee for this).

Review all your transactions. Some will be regular payments, like bills, book club purchases, or groceries, while others will be one-off expenses, like a hotel bill from your last trip to Vegas.

Then, create folders (electronic or physical) for both your income and your expenses. So, for example, if you get paid through electronic deposits, store your paystubs in a folder that is dedicated entirely to paperwork associated with your employment. If you automatically pay for a loan each month, create a folder with everything related to the loan and its associated payments. If you pay gym membership fees, create a folder for everything related to your gym membership. If you travel, put all documentation related to travel, including receipts, in that folder. The idea here is to get highly organized so that you have a clear idea of what's happening to your money each month.

If you're still not sure where all your money is coming from or going to, perhaps you've thrown out every piece of paperwork you've ever received (though this might feel liberating, it's not financially responsible). You should keep all of your statements and receipts for a month or two and then review.

In fact, it is almost always a good idea to keep your receipts. Then, when your bank or credit card statement rolls in at the end of the month, you can cross-reference your pile of receipts with your statement. In two separate instances, I have caught mistakes on my credit card statement this way; the first was a double-charge from a restaurant, and the second was a double-charge at a gas station.

Once you have an idea of where your money is going, you can begin to categorize your expenses in a spreadsheet or other budget template. If you have online banking, you can even download a listing of your expenditures so you don't have to type them out yourself.

YOUR HARD-EARNED DOUGH

Take a second to think about all your sources of income. For many young women, this is very straightforward; you earn a regular salary, and a paycheque is deposited in your bank account. But for others, who perhaps are self-employed, earn on commission, or do freelance work, it can be a little more complicated. To the best of your ability, list out your sources of income.

An example of 33-year-old Penelope's income is listed below. For the past two years, she has worked in the sales department for a medical supply company, and though she works on commission, her after-tax monthly income is fairly predictable. The only time she has a "dip" in her earnings is when she takes holidays and doesn't sell anything for a few weeks. Penelope plans in advance for that downtime by contributing to a savings account, which she uses to level out the dip.

MONTHLY INCOME	TOTAL
Paycheque	$5,100
Sales Bonus	$150
Total Income	**$5,250**

WHAT YOU CAN'T LIVE WITHOUT

Some expenses are necessary evils, meaning you don't have much of a choice when it comes to paying them. These are things like taxes, rent or mortgage payments, insurance, and groceries. Though you may think you might die without your hair extensions, curly, long locks are far from necessary. Round up a list of your crucial expenses and total them in spreadsheet software. Here is an example of a Penelope's necessary monthly expenses.

MONTHLY EXPENSE	TOTAL
Investments (retirement savings)	$250
Savings (to manage the dip in her income)	$250
Mortgage	$1,600
Utilities (heating/cooling, electricity, water, sewage, etc.)	$150
Home Association Fees (condo fees, community fees, etc.)	$100
Insurance (home, car, health, etc.)	$100
Taxes (property and other)	$150
Loan Payment	$300
Credit Card Payment	$500
Groceries	$350
Transportation (fuel, parking, public transit)	$100
Total Necessary Expenses	**$3,850**

You'll note that at the top of Penelope's expenses are savings for her retirement and for managing the dip in her income when she takes holidays. Later in this chapter, you'll learn how important it is to set aside savings for your future, prior to paying any other bills. This is the concept of "paying yourself first," and most millionaire women stress its importance.

NOT-SO-NECESSARY EXPENSES

You guessed it — round up a list of your not-so-necessary expenses and total them in your spreadsheet. These are things like trips to the aesthetician, cell phone bills, cable television, drinks or meals out with friends, vacations, gifts, and gym memberships. Many not-so-necessary expenses are not paid for through automatic banking withdrawals, so it can really help to go through old receipts. Keep this list grouped together and place it below the list of necessary expenses. Penelope's not-so-necessary expenses are listed below.

MONTHLY EXPENSE	TOTAL
Savings for trips	$200
Cell Phone	$60
Internet/Cable	$60
Beautification (hair, nails, spa, etc.)	$100
Donations	$50
Gym Membership	$50
Gifts	$50
Dinners/Drinks/Entertainment	$500
Total Not-So-Necessary Expenses	**$1,070**

GETTING TO THE BOTTOM LINE

Your bottom line is what you have left over when you subtract your total expenses from your total income. When that number is positive, it means you are spending within your budget and have a surplus. When that number is negative, it means you are overspending and running a deficit. If you are spending to the point where you have nothing left each month, you have neither a surplus nor a deficit. In Penelope's case, she has a $330 surplus each month. Have a look at her total monthly budget.

MONTHLY INCOME	TOTAL
Paycheque	$5,100
Sales Bonus	$150
Total Income	**$5,250**

MONTHLY EXPENSE	TOTAL
Investments (retirement savings)	$250
Savings (to manage the dip in her income)	$250
Mortgage	$1,600
Utilities (heating/cooling, electricity, water, sewage, etc.)	$150
Home Association Fees (condo fees, community fees, etc.)	$100
Insurance (home, car, health, etc.)	$100
Taxes (property and other)	$150
Loan Payment	$300
Credit Card Payment	$500
Groceries	$350
Transportation (fuel, parking, public transit)	$100
Total Necessary Expenses	**$3,850**
Savings for trips	$200
Cell Phone	$60
Internet/Cable	$60
Beautification (hair, nails, spa, etc.)	$100
Donations	$50
Gym Membership	$50
Gifts	$50
Dinners/Drinks/Entertainment	$500
Total Not-So-Necessary Expenses	**$1,070**
Total Expenses	**$4,920**
Total Income minus Total Expenses	*$5,250 - $4,920*
BOTTOM LINE	$330

MANAGING A SURPLUS

Having money left over each month is ideal, and on the surface, Penelope's budget looks very healthy because she has a surplus.

However, what you don't know about Penelope is that she likes to shop for the latest concert tickets, electronics, fashion, music, and art trends, and charges her purchases on her credit card — she doesn't operate on the cash system that was discussed in chapter 2, whereby all her purchases would be made with cash rather than credit. Sometimes Penelope spends up to $1,000 on a purchase. The result of her shopping habit is that she now owes $8,000 on her credit card (at a rate of 18 percent interest), which is maxed out, and she only pays $500 per month toward her credit card debt. It will take her 19 months to pay off the debt and cost approximately $1,200 in interest with $500 monthly payments — and that assumes she charges nothing further to her card.

In Penelope's case, she should use her $330 surplus to pay down her credit card balance because it is costing her 18 percent in interest. If she makes monthly credit card payments of $830 rather than $500, it will take 11 months to pay off the debt, and she'll save a little over $500 in interest charges — again, that assumes she charges nothing further on her credit card.

If you're like Penelope and not operating on the cash system, the best way to allocate your surplus is toward making the transition to the cash system. If you still have a surplus once you're on the cash system, and have stopped racking up your credit card and line of credit, there are a variety of ways for you to use your surplus:

- Debt reduction — Make extra payments on your highest-interest debt, as this is the debt that costs the most.

- Savings — Do you have something you want to save up for, like a down payment on a house or tuition for school?

- Investments — Retirement is much closer than you think. You must allocate money toward a retirement savings program.

- Reward yourself — You work very hard for your money, and from time to time it is healthy to treat yourself to something that means a lot to you. For example, I love to travel, and so I like to reward myself with trips to a new part of the world each year. The beautiful thing about rewarding yourself when you have a surplus and are operating on the cash system is that it is relatively guilt-free.

- Combine debt reduction, savings, investments, and rewards — It is entirely possible to allocate your surplus toward all of these. If you choose to split it up, I would still recommend you allocate a larger portion to debt reduction than anything else.

TACKLING A DEFICIT

Think a deficit is no big deal? Think again. Running a monthly deficit in your spending plan will ensure you end up broke and in debt. Wealthy women do not overspend. They live by the cardinal rule that to become financially independent, a woman must spend within her means.

Let's say you're running in the red each month, which explains why your credit card balance keeps rising. You have to make changes in the way that you're spending. Start by reviewing your list of expenses, line by line, and find ways to cut back on or cut out unnecessary things. This is the perfect opportunity to apply the Frugal Fundamentals and move to the cash system (both discussed in chapter 2). Review your larger expenses, ideally to save larger sums of money, and then move to the smaller ones.

Your mortgage or rent payment is probably your largest expense, thus presenting the greatest opportunity to save. Think hard about how much you are spending on your home. Have you overextended yourself? If so, you may have to move to a more affordable location. My sister, for example, moved to London, England, in 2012 with her husband. Not being overly familiar with the neighbourhoods in London, they selected a flat in a hip part of the city. Little did they know how expensive "hip" truly is. Within months they felt financially squeezed and started to hunt around for a less expensive flat. When their lease was up, they moved to their new home, which was a bit smaller, but saved them the equivalent of $600 per month. Opportunities to save on your home exist in every city, not just expensive ones like London, New York, Toronto, Vancouver, Calgary, et cetera.

Do you and your spouse have more than one vehicle? Try to sell one and share the other. You'll save on car payments, fuel, and insurance. Better yet, if you live in a major centre, go car-less. Most large cities have community car-sharing programs like Car2Go and ZipCar for times when you need a vehicle. Otherwise, use other modes of transportation to get around — public transit, cycling, walking, or in-line skating.

Review all your credit cards and loans, including your mortgage, to ensure you are paying the lowest interest rates possible. A quick search on Google will reveal current posted rates for all types of lending products where you live. Shop around and negotiate for the most competitive rates (more on how to negotiate in chapter 4).

Are your insurance premiums higher than average? Speak to an insurance broker and have them present you with a variety of lower rate options that could meet your needs. You can also save on your annual premiums by raising your deductible, the amount of money you must pay to make a claim. For example, six years ago I raised my deductible for my home and auto insurance to $2,000 from $500. That change reduced my annual premium by $250. And because I have never made a claim, over six years I've saved $1,500.

Wondering what the heck you would do if you had to make a claim and come up with the full $2,000 deductible? Well, by the end of this book, you'll know how to build an emergency fund, and $2,000 won't seem like much relative to what you're saving by having the higher deductible.

Cutting back on smaller expenses is easy, too! The old adage "Take care of your pennies, and the dollars will take care of themselves" is based on the idea that you should pay close attention to smaller expenses because they add up to be quite substantial over time. Reduce the number of cable channels you have, make tea at home, review your cell phone plan and provider, get rid of your home phone, shop at discount grocery stores, et cetera. You get the idea — when you are running a deficit, you have to make changes to how you are spending. Some of these changes, like calling your utility provider and re-bundling your services at a lower rate, are easy to make, while others, like not splurging on dinners with friends each week, are harder because they require changes in your lifestyle.

If you decide to change your spending behaviours, don't be surprised if it feels uncomfortable at first. It will take about three or four months before the new behaviours feel normal.

SOCIAL RAMIFICATIONS OF DEALING WITH A DEFICIT

My friend Chelsea has become very careful with her spending because she is diligently chipping away at her debts — a student loan, a car loan, and a personal loan she took out to go travelling with her boyfriend for a year. Whenever our crew gets together, she gives us all an update on the progress she's making with her debt repayment. For her, becoming debt-free is a source of pride, and our friends cheer her on as she gets closer to her goal.

Wondering how your friends are going to react if you stop meeting up each week for a $50 dinner? Don't beat yourself up over it. Just be honest with them about what you're trying to accomplish, and ask for their support. If your pals are true friends, they'll rally behind your efforts to be frugal, and may even join in. Offer up alternative get-together suggestions, like taking turns hosting meals at each other's homes, meeting up for coffee or a glass of wine rather than an expensive meal, or simply reducing the frequency and calibre of dinners out.

If any of them gives you flak for trying to improve your finances, you may want to fire them.

I can't predict how your pals will treat you, but I can certainly assure you that the personal consequences of racking up debt because you can't control your spending will prevent you from achieving many of your goals, like starting a small business or owning a home, and the stress of shouldering buckets of debt will keep you up at night.

PAY THE PRETTY LADY

After paying my way through university, I was so proud of my accomplishment and ecstatic about my future, but once I'd put a small down payment on my home, I was broke and I hated that feeling! So I got serious about saving, knowing that no one but ME was responsible for creating an awesome future for myself.

Because I had a gazillion home-related expenses to pay for, I started saving in small doses *and* before I paid any of my bills. I signed up for my company's retirement savings program and contributed 4 percent of my earnings. This was deducted directly from my paycheque before taxes, preventing me from spending my savings and reducing what I paid in income tax. My company matched 50 percent of my contribution, for total savings of 6 percent of my income. Over six years I grew the percent of my income that I saved each year; 4 percent grew to 6 percent, which grew to 10 percent and eventually to 20 percent. And all the while, I was receiving a proportion of my savings in matched contributions from my employer — free money!!!

It was exciting to watch my savings grow and benefit from the power of compounded interest and reinvested returns. It works like this: Once you begin saving and investing your money, you earn interest and returns on your original investment, which is also known as the principal. Over time, your interest and returns are reinvested, and you earn further interest and returns on your original principal but also on the existing interest and returns. Then you earn interest and returns on the interest and returns on the interest and returns on the principal.... You get the point. This *compounding effect* carries on for as long as your money is invested, so the longer the time you have your money invested, the longer your money benefits from it.

I also like to think of the compounding effect like making a snowball. You stand at the top of a hill in the dead of winter and pack some snow together with your hands until you have a snowball that's the size of a grapefruit. The snow you use to make the snowball is your savings. Once you're satisfied, you let your snowball roll down the long hill. On its way it picks up snow, dirt, twigs, and whatever else it rolls over; this is the interest and returns that your savings earn over time. With each rotation, the surface area of the snowball expands, which is like the reinvestment of your interest and returns. At the bottom of the hill, the once grapefruit-sized snowball is now the size of an exercise ball (like the ones you stretch on at the gym). You've probably guessed this already, but the longer the hill, or time, you give your money to grow, the bigger your snowball becomes — that's the power of compounded interest and reinvested returns. So, the moral of this story is the earlier you start to save, the larger your snowball will be.

There are hundreds of possible priorities for your budget, such as rent, tuition, condominium fees, gym memberships, groceries, fuel for your vehicle, debt repayment, and so many more. But there is nothing as important as setting aside money for your future. Nobody but *you* will save for your future — and it's expensive.

When you prepare your budget, start setting aside some savings before you pay any other bills — that's right — even before you make your rent or mortgage payment. Pay yourself first, before you pay for anything else. The easiest way to pay yourself first is to have your savings automatically deducted from your paycheque or bank account the day you get paid.

My research of wealthy women shows that to really grow their savings, most save 15–20 percent of everything they make (before taxes). I'm not one to reinvent the wheel, so I believe modelling after wealthy women is likely to produce a similar result — savings success!

"Whoa — that's a lot of money," you say. There is no denying that saving 15–20 percent of your earnings is a tall order to fill, but don't get overwhelmed right out of the gate. It takes time to grow your savings, but it's well worth the effort in the end.

Start small. Look closely at your budget and figure out a way to set aside savings. Don't give up if you're financially stretched; even 1 percent is better than 0 percent. If, for example, your gross pay is $2,500 a month, 1 percent in savings would equal $25. Or try setting aside $1 a day, which is $30 a month. Surely you can scrounge up $1 a day — return bottles, make your coffee at home, grow your own veggies, park in a less expensive lot, paint your own toenails, et cetera. Tuck your savings away before you pay for anything else — yes, even before you pay for your son's Scouts fees. The rest of your regular budgeted expenses will adjust to your new savings and be paid for as usual.

As each month passes, try to increase the amount you're saving by small increments. For example, one dollar per day turns into two dollars per day, or 1 percent turns into 2 percent, which turns into 3 percent. As time goes by, you and your budget will adjust to these small increases in the amount that you're saving.

A by-product of paying yourself first is that young women become highly resourceful in managing their budgets. Once they see their savings grow (totally exciting), they become motivated to waste less and save more. Say "ta-ta" to buying a $15 car wash each week — do it yourself twice a month for $4 each time.

PAY THE PIPER

Besides the bare essentials like saving for your future, paying your mortgage and taxes, and putting food on the table, debt repayment is a high priority in budgeting.

Know to whom you owe money (the lender), how much (the balance), the regular required payment, and the interest rate(s) you're paying on your debts. Each debt should be listed separately within your budget. If, for example, you pay a car loan as well as your line of credit each month, list each and the associated monthly payment.

Similar to the principle of increasing the amount you save each month, you'll want to try to find a way to increase the amount you can pay on the highest-interest debt. For example, if the regular payment on your personal loan is $250 each month, and it has the highest interest rate of all your debts, then pay a little extra on that loan. Even $15 can make a big difference in eliminating this debt sooner than you'd planned. It might mean cutting back on a glass of vino with your friends each week, or buying generic-brand food, but paying a little extra will get you into a position where you are debt-free much faster.

Chapter 4 will present a highly effective method of debt repayment, so stay tuned.

HEALTH AND WELLNESS

Your health is very important, and though I have suggested a variety of ways to save money and carefully manage your budget, under no circumstances do I recommend you compromise your health while trying to save a few dollars.

That said, if you're overpaying for a gym membership you rarely use, cut it out of your budget and find a less expensive alternative. If you take medications, research whether there are generic-brand drugs that would satisfactorily fill your prescription.

The idea here is to take care of yourself and feel good about your finances in the process.

CHAPTER 4
Ladies, Lose the Debt

SHE'S IN OVER HER HEAD

Catherine, a carefree overspender, and Miguel, a frugal saver, decided it was time to buy a house. They'd been married for two years, were living in a small apartment, and felt it was time to start building equity in a home rather than "throwing money away" in rent each month. Though Catherine and Miguel had — they thought — excellent communication throughout their relationship, one area they seemed to avoid was household finance. But the desire to own a home meant they had to understand their current financial position. So, they sat down one evening and had a financial tell-all.

Out came the laptops and bank statements. As they pieced together their individual lists of assets and liabilities, it became very clear that Catherine's debts and poor credit history were going to be an issue (this was further validated by their mortgage broker). On top of occasionally being late on making payments, Catherine owed $9,000 on credit cards, $15,000 in consumer loans, and $10,000 in student loans. Miguel, on the other hand, had finished paying off the majority of his debts two years ago (always on time), had built up $12,000 in savings, and owed only $2,000 on his line of credit.

Miguel was angry with Catherine for being financially irresponsible and "wrecking" their chances of owning a home. In his opinion, if she'd simply been responsible rather than gallivanting around at fancy dinners and buying expensive purses, she wouldn't be in this poor financial position. In turn, Catherine blamed Miguel for never making time to talk about money and pushing the subject under the rug.

Financial issues can seriously stress a relationship — and it is so unnecessary.

Until Miguel and Catherine sat down and dug through their finances, Catherine really hadn't given much thought to money management. For the most part, she kept up with her payments and never missed contributing her portion of the regular household expenses. But reviewing her total financial picture revealed she was far from financially secure. For her own personal financial well-being and the sake of her relationship, she was determined to form a plan to improve her finances.

WHEN DEBT GETS IN THE WAY

Debt is a ball and chain around a young woman's ankle. It prevents her from being able to do the things she wants and adds unnecessary stress to her life. In Catherine's case, the dream she had with Miguel to own a home was at risk of vanishing, as was the relationship itself.

When debt gets in the way of being able to afford your future, or if it causes unhealthy stress, it's time to make changes.

GET THE FACTS

Show and tell doesn't stop in grade school; it just gets pricier as we age. Whether you covet your neighbour's turbo-engine lawnmower or your kid sister's vacation property, peer pressure, greed, and easy access to credit perpetuate debt. Whenever you're tempted to overspend, just remember that the Joneses are broke, so there's no point in trying to keep up with them.

Over the past 30 years, the landscape of personal debt has transformed. Not only are young women the fastest-growing segment of independent consumers, their debts are on the rise, too. Additionally, the type of household debt accessed by most consumers has transformed from being tough-to-qualify-for debts secured against a person's property, like mortgages, to easy-to-qualify-for unsecured debts, like car loans, revolving lines of credit, and credit cards. As a result of easy access to credit, household debt as a proportion of income has doubled in nearly every developed country, and in some places has increased by a factor of close to 10.

Think we learned our lesson about the perils of debt from the recent global financial crisis? Unfortunately not. According to a 2013 report from Credit Suisse, consumer debt levels continue to surge across the globe. Countries like Canada and Italy, for example, carried on increasing their debt-to-income ratios despite worsening financial conditions, and today Canada has the highest household debt-to-income ratio among G7 countries. Certainly, there are exceptions, like in the United States and the United Kingdom, where major personal debt–reduction efforts were made post-recession, but on average, the ratio of personal debt to net worth has increased 50 percent around the globe. It should also be noted that much of the decrease in personal debt levels post–financial crisis in the United States relates to foreclosures and financial institution writedowns. Not surprisingly, the highest levels of personal debt are found in developed countries with well-established and sophisticated credit markets.[1]

The Certified General Accountants Association of Canada's annual study on consumer debt, released each May, reported in 2011 that Canadians collectively owed $1.5 trillion, which is nearly three times greater than the amount owed in 1980.[2] Throughout that same period of time, the population increased by only 0.5 times, or 50 percent.[3] In 2013, Canadian consumer debt grew to $1.6 trillion, according to Statistics Canada; of that, $1.1 trillion was mortgage-related, while $500 billion was consumer loans. Thus, the average adult Canadian's personal consumer debt hovers around $27,000 (this figure excludes mortgage debt, but includes what people owe on their credit cards, car loans, installment loans, and lines of credit).[4]

In 2013, Americans owed a total of $11.15 trillion dollars, which is significantly less than the 2008 peak personal debt level of $12.68 trillion. Though Americans appear to be trimming their overall personal debt levels, auto and student loans, along with credit card balances, continue to rise.[5] According to the Federal Reserve, in 2013 the average American household owed over $15,000 on their credit cards, $147,000 in mortgages, and $32,000 in student loans.[6]

In both countries, the most popular form of credit is revolving credit, like lines of credit and credit cards.

The trend of increased borrowing for non-mortgage-related debt is linked to lavish spending, an increasing number of two-income households (and associated overspending), debt accessibility, and affordable interest rates. Some experts believe that our attitudes toward debt have shifted; rather than using debt to build net worth, we use it to fuel our desire to act richer than we truly are.

Surely, we're happier than our debt-free grandparents? False. Sadly, even though our houses are bigger and our cars fancier, we're no happier than previous generations. Debt contributes to dissatisfaction because it is expensive, restrictive, and detrimental to health and personal relationships. On average, couples have at least five money fights each year.[7]

Besides hugging your pet and taking 10 deep breaths each day, the best ways to relieve money-related stress are to reduce debt and live within your means.

MANAGE THE GOOD, ELIMINATE THE BAD

Since avoiding debt completely seems nearly impossible these days, the best strategy is to borrow only to invest in assets (good debt), and avoid debts that don't help increase your net worth (bad debt).

In moderation, good debt helps build net worth through owning a home with a mortgage, building a business through a small-business loan, supporting your education with student loans, or investing in retirement using a retirement savings loan. These investments are expected to grow in value, which is why they are categorized by the term *assets*. You'll note a couple of unique things about this list: first, vehicles don't appear, and second, education is considered an asset even though it's often accompanied by student loans.

Vehicles are not considered assets. They never have been and never will be. Don't be fooled — though your car salesperson will say otherwise, your automobile will *never, ever* increase in value, and you will *never, ever* make money on it. Along with furniture and electronics, cars are one of the fastest-depreciating pieces of property you can own. Sure, they are useful in that they get you from point A to point B, but that's where their benefits end. Unless you own some fancy-schmancy, antique collector's car, I can one-hundred-percent guarantee that your vehicle's value will plummet the moment you drive it off the lot. Therefore, loans associated with cars are bad debts.

Education, on the other hand, is an asset because with an education your income-earning ability and lifestyle choices are far greater than those of someone without one. Chapter 5 will discuss further how much more an educated young woman will make over the course of her lifetime than an uneducated young woman. Though student loans are painful when a young woman first graduates, they are considered good debts because education is an asset.

To make the most of good debt, start by determining if the asset is stable and expected to grow. For example, research the neighbourhood where you're thinking of buying a home: job market, schools, development plans, projected growth. If all factors indicate that the home is likely to increase in value long term, it's considered an asset, and taking out a mortgage to finance the property would be wise.

Next, secure an interest rate that is lower than the expected long-term growth rate on the asset. If, based on historical and current real estate statistics, the house is expected to appreciate 6 percent annually, get a mortgage at 5 percent. You'll realize the benefit of increased property value, plus the principal reduction of the mortgage adds equity value. Don't worry about rising interest rates. Despite an improving economy, interest rates still remain competitive and payment plans flexible.

No one has a crystal ball to determine exactly what will happen to real estate prices, but good research should point you in the right direction in terms of a home's or community's potential to maintain or grow in value. A real estate professional can help supply this type of information.

Third, make regular payments, and avoid borrowing back the principal through refinancing or a line of credit. The only way your good debts become bad debts is if you never pay them off. The perils of seductive lines of credit will be discussed later in this chapter.

Bad debts, like credit cards and consumer loans used to purchase depreciating assets, don't build your net worth. If you're guilty of justifying your Hugo Boss suit as a good debt, thinking it'll contribute to your job promotion at work, think again.

If it's on your *ass*, it's not an *asset*!

Your suit will never increase in value, and it's highly unlikely that a job promotion will come your way unless you're a stellar performer at work. So put away your credit card, leave the Nordstrom store, and instead invest your time in making yourself invaluable to your employer — hard work, professionalism, and smart career planning will pay off down the road. Now, I'm not suggesting you show up to work looking like a hobo. Try to strike a balance between dressing like a professional, without breaking the bank, and executing your job responsibilities well.

Bad debts are considered liabilities, and you should avoid them. Interest rates on bad debts are often quite high, and payment plans are restrictive. Thus, the best way to handle bad debt is to get rid of it as quickly and efficiently as possible using the "Crush It" system described next.

USE YOUR YOUNG-WOMAN SUPERPOWER AND "CRUSH IT"

Throughout the past few years, I've researched how young women manage debt relative to their male counterparts. You'll be relieved to know that, despite the scary-big amounts of debt young women are carrying these days, they are far better and faster at ridding themselves of their debts than their male peers are. According to many studies, including one released by the credit bureau Experian, though women earn, on average, 20 percent less than men, they are better at reducing their debts and managing their credit scores.[8,9] Some university studies claim that women are better at debt reduction due to their inherent biological nature to be more risk-averse. Risk aversion also plays into the greater conservatism and higher returns displayed among women investors, as will be discussed in chapter 7.

Whatever the reason, we should use our debt-reduction superpowers to shed bad debts as quickly as possible, saving us money and lowering stress.

I've developed a debt-reduction system for young women called "Crush It," and below is a summary of the strategy.

Step 1: Remove the temptation to spend. The idea behind this is to break the cycle of overspending and accumulating debt before it even starts. For example, don't go to the mall if you're likely to buy a new set of rims for your car. Take your name off promotional lists and online coupon websites. Reduce your available credit and have only one credit card.

Step 2: Get organized. Knowing who you owe, how much, the interest rates, and the regular payments is key. Once you know where you stand, you can execute the rest of the Crush It strategy.

Step 3: Negotiate your interest rates. You can save thousands of dollars by negotiating for the lowest rates on your debts. It doesn't take long, either — 10 minutes per lender will suffice.

Step 4: Pay a little extra on the highest-interest debt. It costs the most. Cut back by a few drinks or muffins each week so you can pay more — even $10 makes a difference. Once you've paid off the highest-interest debt, move on to the next.

Step 5: Don't incur additional debt while tackling the existing debt. This is probably the most important step. Can you imagine how dreadful it would be if you spent two years executing the Crush It strategy, only to have to do it again? That would be brutal! If you don't rein in your spending, you'll never get out from under it, so you have to make money-saving changes to your lifestyle to stop the debt-accumulation cycle.

The next section provides details for each step of the Crush It system.

STEP 1: REMOVE THE TEMPTATION TO SPEND

I am a sucker for home decorating. If I had no self-control, I would probably paint my home annually and swap out the art, furniture, and kitchen appliances twice a year. I know that walking into a home decor store or looking at furniture on Kijiji are my kryptonite, so I don't do those things unless I genuinely need something ... and upgrading my crystal wine glasses doesn't count as a "need." To ensure I'm not tempted, I even go so far as to steer clear of areas in the city where home decorating stores are huddled together in close proximity.

What's your spending kryptonite? If you generally splurge on the deals for trips, shoes, or patio furniture that pop up in your inbox each morning, take your name off promotional lists. That's right — you need to hit that dreadful little button at the bottom of your emails that says *unsubscribe*.

"But what if I need the item that's being promoted?" you say. If you are absolutely, a-thousand-percent sure you need something, most stores offer online downloadable coupons on demand. So don't fret — with a little Internet surfing, you'll still have access to great deals. Likewise, if you have a nasty habit of trading in your car each year for the latest model (by the way, this is ridiculously un-frugal, especially if you don't receive a car allowance through work), don't go to the car show.

Besides having only one credit card, to further reduce the temptation to spend, lower your available credit limits on your line of credit and credit card. So, let's say your line of credit limit is $40,000, and you currently owe $34,000; reduce your limit to $34,000, and as you pay down the line of credit, continue to collapse down the limit so you can't borrow any more money.

STEP 2: GET ORGANIZED

You can't successfully crush your debts unless you know who you owe money to, and the interest rate, balance, and required payment of each debt. Using a handy-dandy spreadsheet or piece of graph paper, gather a detailed list of your debts (and your partner's debts, if you have one) and record them in descending interest-rate order. You also need to take into account unofficial loans, like the $1,000 you owe your sister from when you borrowed money last year to make rent. If you promised to pay her back, you need to either keep your promise or ask her to forgive the loan; otherwise, it's the equivalent of stealing money, which is not cool.

If you're not sure about your list of debts, dig out your statements and lay them on your kitchen table. Once you've collected the whole lot, then you can organize the pile of statements from left to right in descending interest-rate order.

Let's go back to the story at the beginning of the chapter and apply this concept. Catherine owes $9,000 on credit cards, $15,000 in consumer loans, and $10,000 in student loans. In her spreadsheet, she lists her various debts, and the interest rate, the balance, and her regular monthly payment for each one.

	Visa	MasterCard	Consumer Loan (local bank)	Student Loan (local bank)
Rate	19%	18%	13%	6%
Balance	$4,000	$5,000	$15,000	$10,000
Fixed Monthly Payment	$300	$200	$350	$350

Notice that Catherine has listed her debts from left to right in order of descending interest rate.

STEP 3: NEGOTIATE YOUR INTEREST RATES

Ladies, get your pretty game faces on! It's time to have a tough conversation with your lenders.

Just for a brief moment, think football. Like an outside lineman protecting his star quarterback, you need to fight hard to protect your net worth. No, you won't get a chance to tackle your lender, but a good negotiation to lower your interest rates can save you thousands of dollars, which will help you pay off your debts faster and grow your bottom line.

If, for example, you owe $8,000 on your credit card at 19 percent interest, and pay $250 a month, it'll take approximately 45 months to pay it off. If, however, you negotiate your rate to 10 percent, it'll take 38 months to pay it off and you'll save close to $2,000 in interest charges. If you're wondering what your debts are costing you, check out GetSmarterAboutMoney.com or BankRate.com for cost-of-borrowing calculators on car loans, credit cards, mortgages, and other personal loans.

The best part about negotiating is that it shouldn't take you more than 10 minutes per lender. When you're on the phone or meeting with your lender, follow this negotiation process:

1) Get prepared by ensuring you have the most up-to-date information on the terms, balance, and rate of your loan.

2) Next, research current rates by reviewing the websites of various lenders, along with the following:

In Canada
- For mortgages: *www.ratehub.ca*

- For credit cards: *http://creditcards.redflagdeals.com* (index of credit card rates and annual fees) or *www.creditcards.ca*
- For general current interest rate information: *www.bankofcanada.ca*

In the United States

- For all types of loans and credit cards in your area: *www.bankrate.com*
- For credit cards: *www.indexcreditcards.com* (compares all cards, their perks and rates)

If you live outside of these countries, a quick Google search for rates in your area will do the trick.

3) Call your lenders, one by one, speak to a representative or manager, and ask for a better rate. Remember, if you don't ask, you don't get! Keep what you researched in mind during your discussions. Most credit grantors will try to work with you to keep your business, especially if you're a good client. Generally speaking, I'd recommend targeting at least a 5–10 percent decrease on credit card interest rates and a 2–5 percent decrease on all other consumer loans. Mortgages can be more difficult to negotiate (re-financing), as they are typically locked in for longer terms — still, investigate whether it's a worthwhile option for you.

   Be prepared to present a competitive offer that your lender could potentially match.

4) If the lender doesn't want to reduce your rate, prepare to take your business elsewhere.

Caution! Sometimes lenders will try to saddle you with fees and penalties for renegotiating. Just be aware that these extra costs are also negotiable, and, whatever you do, ensure the benefits of renegotiation outweigh the costs (especially with the renegotiation of a mortgage).

Negotiating interest rates may seem daunting, but it isn't; remember that a 10-minute phone call can save you thousands of dollars. Why pay extra interest when you can save money through a simple negotiation with your lender?

Going back to the previous example, because Catherine can't qualify for a consolidation loan (details on this later in the chapter) due to her poor credit history, she's left with having to repay her debt the good, old-fashioned way: multiple payments to multiple lenders. So, she gets on the phone with her lenders to negotiate the best possible interest rates. She successfully lowers her Visa, MasterCard, and consumer-loan rates, but not the rate on her student loan. Her revised list of debts looks as follows:

	Visa	MasterCard	Consumer Loan (local bank)	Student Loan (local bank)
Rate	18%	12%	11%	6%
Balance	$4,000	$5,000	$15,000	$10,000
Fixed Monthly Payment	$300	$200	$350	$350

STEP 4: PAY A LITTLE EXTRA ON THE HIGHEST-INTEREST DEBT

Feel better after flexing your negotiating muscles? Great! Now, focus on paying off the highest-interest debt first, because it costs the most. In order to do that using the Crush It system, you'll need to pay a little extra on the most expensive debt every month while continuing to make regular payments on your other debts. Even $20 extra makes a difference.

Where's the "extra" money going to come from? By applying the Frugal Fundamentals from chapter 2 to your spending. Cut back on your number of coffees each week, stop buying music and listen to CDs from the library, or puppy-sit on the weekends.

As an alternative, another easy way to pay extra is to set up accelerated weekly or biweekly (every two weeks) payments. These payments allow you to tack on a little extra with each payment automatically. Say, for example, your regular payment on a loan is $225 biweekly. An accelerated biweekly payment would be slightly higher, like $240. That extra $15 is built right into your payment, which automatically gets deducted from your bank account every two weeks. Naturally, the rest of your personal spending adjusts to accommodate that tiny bit extra. And because it's automatically deducted from your account, ideally on payday, you'll hardly notice that tiny amount is gone.

Though some financial experts claim accelerated payments are magical — poof, your debts are gone nearly instantly — there is nothing magic about them. You're simply paying a little extra automatically, and some young women find that a bit easier. That's all there is to it.

To set up accelerated payments, simply call your lender and ask. Note that in many cases, however, accelerated payment options are not readily available for credit cards because only the minimum payment is due each month, which is generally 2 to 6 percent of the balance or $10, whichever is higher. If you make only minimum payments on your credit card, it will take a very long time to pay off your balance. So don't pay only the minimum; pay more.

You can manage your own credit card repayment independently through online banking by setting up automatic accelerated payments from your bank account on payday. Or call your credit card company and have them automatically debit your chequing account every week or two weeks with the amount you'd like to pay toward the balance.

Whether you scrounge around to find a few extra dollars to put toward your debt each month, or set up accelerated payments, the results are the same: paying a bit extra on your debts will reduce the principal faster than making only regular payments.

Once you've paid off your highest-interest debt, move on to the next highest. Only this time, you'll have the extra money you're no longer using to make minimum payments on the highest-rate debt — and you'll still be paying a little extra through accelerated payments or by cutting out unnecessary expenses.

Back to Catherine for a moment. She has a very tight monthly budget. In fact, between her contribution to the household expenses and her debt payments, she has almost nothing left over each month, so she carefully reviews her monthly spending to find opportunities to save. She re-bundles the household utilities into one provider, saving $50 a month; cuts back her dinners out with Miguel, saving another $50 a month; and eliminates her polish changes that cost $25 a month, for a total of $125 a month in savings.

Each month Catherine takes her $125 in savings and pays a little extra on the highest-interest debt, which in her case is the Visa. Because credit cards charge interest on a daily basis, which is what makes them financially lethal, Catherine applies this extra payment approximately two weeks after her regular monthly payment, to break up the daily interest rate cycle (more on this concept later).

When the Visa is finally paid off, she takes the regular payment from the Visa and the extra $125 in cash and applies both to the debt with the next-highest interest rate, the MasterCard. Once the MasterCard is paid off, Catherine takes the old

WELL-HEELED

regular payment from the Visa, the old regular payment from the MasterCard, and the extra $125 in cash savings and applies them to the consumer loan. As you have probably guessed by now, once the consumer loan is paid off, Catherine takes all the previous regular monthly payments from the Visa, MasterCard, and consumer loan, plus the $125 in cash savings, and applies all that money to the final, lowest-interest debt, her student loan.

Because Catherine commits to not accruing any further debts while paying off her existing debts, she is completely debt-free in approximately two and a half years. Using the Crush It system you can see her balances at the end of each year in the chart below:

	Visa	MasterCard	Consumer Loan (local bank)	Student Loan (local bank)
Rate	18%	12%	11%	6%
Starting Balance	$4,000	$5,000	$15,000	$10,000
Fixed Monthly Payment	$300	$200	$350	$350
Year 1 Ending Balance	$0	$2,200	$12,300	$6,300
Year 2 Ending Balance	$0	$0	$4,100	$2,300
Year 3 Ending Balance	$0	$0	$0	$0

If Catherine doesn't use the Crush It system, meaning she doesn't negotiate her interest rates nor does she pay extra on her loans, it would have taken her close to five years to be completely debt free and cost her an additional $3,300 in interest. See her balances at the end of each year in the chart below:

	Visa	MasterCard	Consumer Loan (local bank)	Student Loan (local bank)
Rate	19%	18%	13%	6%
Starting Balance	$4,000	$5,000	$15,000	$10,000
Fixed Monthly Payment	$300	$200	$350	$350
Year 1 Ending Balance	$900	$3,300	$12,600	$6,300
Year 2 Ending Balance	$0	$1,400	$9,800	$2,300
Year 3 Ending Balance	$0	$0	$6,700	$0
Year 4 Ending Balance	$0	$0	$3,100	$0
Year 5 Ending Balance	$0	$0	$0	$0

Holla! By using the Crush It system, Catherine and Miguel's dream of home ownership will come to fruition twice as fast, *and* Catherine can use her savings in interest toward the down payment on their new house.

You can be just like Catherine — become debt-free faster and save thousands of dollars just by paying a little extra and exercising discipline.

Check out my website, *www.lesleyscorgie.com*, for further details.

STEP 5: DON'T INCUR ADDITIONAL DEBT

As I previously mentioned, the worst thing you can possibly do while applying the Crush It system to your debts is incur more debt. No matter how great the temptation to buy that new-model car is, *do not* rack up added debts while tackling the existing ones. It completely defeats the whole point of debt reduction and perpetuates being broke.

In a nutshell, the Crush It system boils down to getting organized, securing the best interest rates, paying a little extra, and avoiding the accumulation of further debt. It works great for young women, just like you, because it plays off of your strengths — organization, diligence, and hard work.

TO CONSOLIDATE OR GO AT IT THE OLD-FASHIONED WAY

Wondering where consolidation loans fit into the picture? If you're in debt to multiple lenders and yet are managing to make regular payments on the debt (hence, you have a good credit history — more on that later in this chapter), you typically have the choice to either tough out debt repayment the old-fashioned way, like Catherine did (regular payments to multiple lenders) or apply for a consolidation loan (one consolidated monthly payment to one lender).

A consolidation loan places all your debts into one loan at a lower interest rate, allowing you to make one monthly payment instead of multiple payments. A by-product of a lower interest rate is lower monthly payments — but don't get too excited about low payments, because the less you pay, the longer it takes to pay off your consolidation loan.

Most consolidation loans are secured (meaning that you've posted collateral) against an asset such as your house. Secured loans have lower rates than unsecured loans (no collateral posted). If you choose the path of a consolidation loan and you don't have collateral, you can still work with your lender to get the lowest possible rate by emphasizing your good credit.

Many experts rail against consolidation loans because they don't teach the valuable lesson of taking full responsibility for debt accumulation. The act of having to pay off expensive debts the old-fashioned way often imposes enough financial hardship on people that they change their spending habits. Statistics also show that the majority of individuals with consolidation loans never learn their lesson and are first in line for another one when the previous is finished.

You're a good candidate for a consolidation loan if you are paying too much in interest or if you are having a hard time keeping up with regular payments. The first caveat, however, is that you must be financially disciplined and commit to making payments on time and in full, and to not accumulating additional debts. The second caveat is that these loans are difficult to qualify for, since most people who are maxed out are considered high risk.

Many young women turn to lines of credit as pseudo-consolidation loans. Scary! Though interest rates are attractive, lines of credit are revolving; thus, the available borrowing room never decreases. Statistics show that rarely do young women pay off their lines of credit. Rather, they use them to continue overspending, often decreasing home equity. If you do choose to use a line of credit to consolidate, as you pay it down, reduce the borrowing limit.

Consolidation loans are offered at most financial institutions. But again, the key with a consolidation loan is discipline — don't accumulate further debt. You don't want to spend four years paying off your loan, and then have to get another one because you haven't been responsible with your money throughout that time.

THE 411 ON CREDIT CARDS

Credit cards are a convenient way — too convenient — to pay for things, whether or not you can afford them. They're useful when paying tuition, paying for regular home maintenance, purchasing tickets online, booking hotels, renting cars, reserving tables at restaurants, paying medical expenses, or making payments over the phone. The truth is, to function in today's society you need a credit card. When managed properly, credit cards are a useful tool. If you charge an item to your card and don't carry a balance, you've got 30 days to pay it off without paying interest on the purchase.

If, however, you can't pay off the balance, your credit card company will charge interest — typically 17–22 percent — on your purchase. Remarkably, many store credit cards charge even higher interest rates — some in the range of 28 or 29 percent. If you charge a purchase on your credit card while carrying an existing balance, there is usually a 21-day grace period before you'll be charged interest. This grace period varies depending on the card.

Because of high credit limits and the temptation to spend, a balance can accumulate quickly, and it's difficult to pay off for four reasons: first, high interest rates; second, credit card companies set minimum payments between 2 and 6 percent of the outstanding balance (or $10, whichever is highest), which barely covers the interest charges on the card; third, interest is calculated daily, not monthly; and fourth, as you pay off your credit card balance, your minimum payment declines because it's set at a percentage of the balance. Since some consumers make only the minimum payment, this extends the time it takes to pay off the balance.

Suppose you purchase a desk for your home office and charge $1,000 on your credit card at 19 percent interest. The minimum payment on the bill is likely 2 percent of your total balance, meaning $20. If you were to stick to paying only $20 each month, it would take you 100 months to pay off that $1,000. Even worse, you'd pay $997 in interest — you could have purchased two desks for that amount of money!

Deal with credit card debt using the Crush It system by having only one card and reducing the credit limit, negotiating for the best rate, paying a little extra each month, and making payments more frequently to break the interest rate cycle and reduce the principal faster. *And don't rack up additional charges!*

With the exception of owing money to a loan shark, credit card debt is the worst kind of debt. It is financially lethal for the reasons described above, so get rid of it quickly, and from now on use your credit card only as a tool to help build net worth, not erode it!

BEWARE OF SEDUCTIVE LINES OF CREDIT

In 2013, Anane met with her banker to collapse her home equity line of credit (HELOC) and roll it into a refinanced fixed low-rate mortgage. She explained she wasn't getting ahead because the line of credit was too easily accessible and she kept dipping in.

"But you'll be thankful for it when it comes time to renovate," the bank representative responded.

Frustrated that her bank was encouraging her to carry revolving credit, Anane contacted an independent mortgage broker, who consolidated her line of credit and secured a low-rate mortgage, resulting in savings of over $6,000. Anane closed out all her business with her bank.

According to recent reports released by the Certified General Accountants Association of Canada, Canadian households borrow approximately 60 cents for every dollar they spend using revolving credit — credit cards and lines of credit. Due to the lower interest rates on lines of credit relative to credit cards, borrowing using lines of credit has increased 25 times since 1989, contributing to Canada's ranking first among 20

Organization for Economic Co-operation and Development (OECD) countries for highest debt-to-asset ratio — and this is a long-term trend.[10]

The United States is no different. According to the credit bureau, Equifax, and JPMorgan Chase, despite the economic slowdown, Americans continue to use their homes and other assets as ATM machines through lines of credit. The average line of credit in the United States is $90,000, with borrowers collectively withdrawing $7.2 billion in funds in 2012. As the economy improved in 2013, borrowing increased.[11]

Sadly, across North America, lines of credit are rarely paid off. Rather, they're used by customers similarly to credit cards: borrow money, pay some of it back, borrow again, pay some of it back, and so on. Lines of credit revolve, meaning the credit that is available to the consumer never decreases like a traditional loan. Hence, banks make loads of money off them and encourage customers to take out a line of credit before offering up the option of a traditional loan. This explains the response Anane received from her banker.

Lines of credit are masked as good debt because they offer seductively low rates and have flexible repayment options. However, in recent years statistics have shown that North Americans are using lines of credit to live beyond their means. Unless lines of credit are used to purchase assets, which are expected to grow, *and* they're paid off quickly, they are actually bad debt.

Because they're easy to qualify for and access, sometimes even through an ATM card, lines of credit encourage accumulation, layering on more, which translates into bad debt — a deal you can't afford. There's no pressure from the bank to pay off the principal; simply cover the interest. You can even borrow back everything you pay toward it — hence, the revolving aspect of the loan.

Take, for example, a 35-year-old young woman and her partner living beyond their means. They rack up $60,000 on a HELOC from a $10,000 renovation, a $10,000 credit card balance, and a $40,000 vehicle purchase. The low-rate line of credit didn't solve the systemic overspending problem, it facilitated it!

Ladies, unless you're up to your eyeballs in expensive consumer debt (rates north of 10 percent when combined) and are highly disciplined, lines of credit don't make sense; saving in advance does. And forget about unsecured lines of credit (no collateral posted). They're often as expensive as, or more expensive than, a traditional loan.

In this era of consumerism, it's considered blasphemous not to keep pace with your neighbour's spending, financed predominantly by lines of credit. So we need a reality check! If we don't learn how to keep and grow our money, we'll never be financially independent. This means reducing debt, not disguising it with a line of credit.

You know you're abusing your line of credit if: you can justify busting your budget for unplanned purchases like a new TV because you've got a low rate; your bottom line isn't growing, but your line of credit balance is; your credit card is racked up each month because of overspending, and you pay it off with a line of credit rather than cash; you find yourself unable to stop the $5,000 home renovation in the bathroom, and it creeps into new floors, cupboards and sparkling state-of-the-art appliances for the kitchen; or you're expediting the purchase time frame on major items like a car.

Get off the line of credit merry-go-round. It's en vogue to pay off debt.

Lines of credit should be used for good debt only — to invest in stable assets like homes, education, investments, and businesses. Don't confuse home repairs with unnecessary renovations, and avoid investment-market speculation for stocks or real estate. Forget about buying a downtown spec home because your brother said it'd appreciate 200 percent; the red-hot real estate days are gone. Speculation has a tendency to backfire. Thus, it's bad debt.

It's also counterproductive to borrow back what you pay in principal on your line of credit. Change your repayment plan so that the available credit reduces by the same amount as your payment, in essence turning it into a traditional loan.

Consider collapsing your HELOC into a fixed mortgage. Rates are historically low and they won't stay there forever. Payments are more powerful on a 6-percent mortgage than on an 8-percent loan with a five-year term.

Track your progress by monitoring your net worth every month as described in chapter 1. If you live with a spouse or partner, hold each other accountable to your goals of reducing your line of credit balance.

Line of credit accumulation acts, looks, and feels like good debt. But even if you have room on your line of credit, bad debt has zero return on investment — even though a consumer quick-hit, like a drug, might make you temporarily happy, it will only last until the latest-and-greatest product hits the market.

I only recommend lines of credit in the case of a home emergency, when you need immediate access to cash. A $5,000–$10,000 limit is more than sufficient — and do not attach it to your ATM card.

DESPERATE TIMES CALL FOR DESPERATE MEASURES

Sometimes, young women are in so deep they need unconventional measures to get rid of their debts. If this is you and you're having trouble keeping up with your payments, pay attention.

First off, you should seek the help of a credit counsellor. Most credit counselling agencies are non-profit and backed by the government. Their role is to organize your debts and negotiate new repayment terms with your lenders. They will help you to navigate through the best financial alternatives for your circumstances and to avoid bankruptcy and foreclosure. Bankruptcy and foreclosure hurt both you and the credit provider, so try to work with your creditors to arrive at a potential solution. They'll be more willing to negotiate with you if you're serious about paying up, and they'll avoid writing off a bad loan.

Next, you may need to sell your personal possessions in order to reduce your debts. Though it might be emotionally painful to do so, put your car and massage table up for sale online. Get rid of anything in your home that is of value. Pull Junior out of private school and put him in the public system. If things are really bad, you may need to go live with your parents or a sibling for a while, saving you rent or mortgage payments.

On the flip side, you may also need to get yourself a second job.

The point here is that you're going to have to go to great lengths to rid yourself of these hefty debt loads as quickly and efficiently as possible.

KICK YOUR SHOPAHOLIC ADDICTION

Overcoming a shopping addiction, like any addiction, is not easy. But, you can definitely kick it through practical measures such as avoiding places where you can shop, cutting up credit cards, spending your time doing free activities like exercising and other suggestions described in this chapter.

On the emotional side though, it is often very helpful to seek professional counselling regardless of how severe you believe your shopping addiction may be. Counselling can help you to understand, and deal with, the root cause of your addiction, be it boredom, a need for attention, or repeating familial behaviours.

Dealing with the root of the issue is the only sure fire way to permanently overcome the addiction.

Credit counselling centres offer this type of counselling support. Look up agencies near you and set up an appointment.

KNOW YOUR SCORE

Your credit score can impact your ability to borrow, buy a home or car, and even get a job. It reflects your level of financial responsibility; therefore, you must diligently protect it. And because of increased fraud and identity theft, it's equally important that you ensure your credit report is accurate.

Build a strong credit rating through these guidelines:

- Your credit score starts to build the moment you apply for credit. If you pay back your loans on time, responsibly maintain revolving credit (credit cards or lines of credit), and do not declare bankruptcy, you'll build a strong credit rating.

- If you're a co-applicant on a credit card or loan, or if your name isn't directly on a bill, you do not build credit. If you want to build a positive credit record, have your own credit card and loans, put bills in your name, and pay your debts on time.

- If you've damaged your credit score through late payments or not paying a lender back in full, you'll have to repair your credit rating. The only way to repair a bad credit score is to prove you're responsible with money and wait it out, so make your payments on time, don't miss payments, and don't "not pay."

- Be wary of credit counselling agencies that are not endorsed by the government. Although they may claim to "fix" your credit by having bad things removed from your file (in exchange for payments), that's impossible. Unless there is a reporting error on your credit file, your credit score can't be manipulated.

- There are three main credit bureaus in North America that monitor credit scores: Equifax (*www.equifax.com*), Experian (*www.experian.com*), and TransUnion (*www.transunion.com*). You can request a *free* copy of your credit score annually by visiting their websites. Follow these tips when reviewing your credit score:

  o To ensure your credit file has accurate information, check it every year.
  o Confirm that the credit bureau's records match your records. Look for identity theft, corporate reporting errors, loan defaults, and other negative items.
  o If you have a question or inquiry, send a written request (with official receipts and paperwork) to the credit bureau and they will investigate the matter for you.
  o If an error is discovered in your file, the credit bureau must correct it.
  o If an error is corrected, the credit bureau will send copies of the updated file to the credit grantors if you request it.
  o If you've applied for credit and your application is refused, the credit bureau isn't responsible for the decision — the credit grantor makes the decision based on their lending policies. If

you're shut down, you'll be directed to contact the credit bureau to review the information that contributed to the decision.

- Again, if you're struggling to keep up with debt payments, see a credit counsellor.

Good debt in moderation can help you build wealth, but when debt gets in the way of being able to afford the lifestyle you truly want, it's time to make changes to your spending habits. The next chapter will give you plenty of great ideas to help boost your cash flow, which can then be used to help pay off expensive debts.

CHAPTER 5
Pumped-Up Cash Flow

AN INFURIATING INCIDENT

A few years into my working career, I took a great job as an analyst at an energy company. Approximately one year into the job, it was time for my performance and compensation review. I had been working my tail off and I knew that, based on the communication I'd received from management throughout the year, I was exceeding their expectations.

I sat down with my supervisor for my review, and he went through the motions of thanking me for my work and tremendous efforts in bringing together a number of successful projects. He then handed me my compensation letter, which contained my salary and bonus information. Without looking at the header, my eyes darted to the salary and bonus line. I was shocked! I was getting a $16,000 raise, and my bonus was approximately $5,000 higher than I had been expecting. "Wow — thank you!" I said to my boss. He replied by thanking me again for my hard work.

Then, as I got up to leave his office, seemingly out of nowhere he popped out of his chair, grabbed the letter from my hands, and sheepishly said, "Oh no — I've given you the wrong letter! This is Ryan's letter. I'm so sorry, Lesley-Anne, here's your letter." My letter offered a raise of $5,000 and a bonus that was in line with my expectations.

I was really disappointed, but I understood the error. However, when I got home later that day, after thinking about it further, I was super mad. Why was it that my male colleague, with the exact same number of years of experience, was making so much more than I was? In fact, we'd graduated from the exact same university program, at the same school, in the same year only a few years before.

YOUR INCOME: A BATTLE WORTH FIGHTING FOR

I find it frustrating, and I hope you do too, that even in developed countries today, women still make less than men for doing the same jobs. Don't believe me? Statistics don't lie. The World Economic Forum, Conference Board of Canada, and American Community Survey by the U.S. Census Bureau confirm the dismal statistics that women make approximately 20 percent less than men in North America. And that number isn't expected to improve in the near future.[1]

Ladies, let's not become this statistic!

Fighting to protect and grow your income along with advancing your career is important because both money and experience will strengthen the financial and career pillars that support your future, as described in the introductory chapter. Making more money and standing up for your income is also important because it strengthens character, increases personal pride, and improves your reputation. If you recall from the first chapter, millionaire women state that making more money is key to their financial success, along with savvy spending, investing, and giving.

This chapter focuses first on how to stand up for yourself and your income in the workplace (i.e., get a raise) without irritating your boss or being arrogant, and second, how you can increase your income.

COMMUNICATE CLEARLY

Being successful at earning a raise and or getting a promotion starts with clear communication. Women often shy away from tooting their own horns at work. But ladies, you have to in order to get ahead financially. The key to earning more money hinges on your ability to effectively communicate your successes to the decision-makers in your organization. This doesn't mean ratting out colleagues about their poor performances relative to your own. It's about showcasing tangible successes in your work and communicating the value you've brought to the organization.

However, before you blurt out how great your talents are, consider your audience and the timing of your message. If your boss likes facts and numbers, you'll want to gather and present information that supports what you're saying. Try to avoid springing an impromptu meeting on your extremely busy manager as it may iritate them. Set up an appointment to talk about your work. Better yet, push for regular monthly or quarterly performance reviews during which you can communicate your accomplishments in private. These meetings are also an opportunity to discuss your career goals, which shows initiative, and how your current work can support the achievement of those goals.

As the conversation unfolds, present specific examples of your work. Be clear, confident, and stick to the facts. When the topic of your future development and career plans rolls around, clearly articulate where you'd like to see yourself going, and jointly, with your boss, discuss ways to support your development plan. For example, if you want to become a teacher-librarian rather than teaching only math, you may want to arrange to job shadow the current teacher-librarian. It's helpful to write out what you want to say in advance of any performance discussion.

A clear, confident, and assertive approach to communicating your successes isn't boastful or arrogant. It's factual and financially prudent.

ADD VALUE

Many organizations have pay-for-performance compensation systems, whereby employees are rewarded based on their performance. If you're posturing yourself for a raise, ensure that your work contributes to the success of your organization. If you're in a sales role, for example, you'll want to hit your sales targets consistently. If your work isn't directly linked to revenue generation, you'll want to add value through supporting your management team.

Better yet, find ways to save money and build your company's bottom line through higher revenues and lower costs. One of my friends, for example, works as a merchandise sales specialist, and when she's not visiting her retail locations, she's always working on models to try to find opportunities to save money on inventory and generate greater revenues by replacing low-margin products with higher-margin products. Her extra effort and bottom-line-building strategies are what make her a top producer, which equates to higher bonuses relative to her peers.

INVEST IN YOUR EDUCATION AND SKILLS

Wondering whether a college, university, trade school, technical school, or other post-secondary education is a good investment? Considering 75 percent of future jobs will require education past high school, the answer is *yes!*[2] In addition, according to Statistics Canada and CIBC World Markets and a 2013 report from the U.S. Census Bureau entitled "The Big Payoff," when you invest in any type of education past high school, your long-term income-earning ability is a few hundred thousand dollars to over a million dollars greater than a high school graduate's.[3,4] Though the short-term pains of student loans may seem unbearable, it's worth the long-term gains in income throughout your working career.

Research has also shown that educated women not only earn more money, but also enjoy a higher quality of life because they have more choices in terms of their career opportunities and lifestyle.

Investing in your education will also give you a competitive edge in the workplace. You'll have new skills to apply to your job, and you'll benefit from broader thinking, which is at the core of any education.

Going back to school full-time while you're in the midst of your career is difficult. If you leave the workforce, you'll forfeit your income and experiences for the time you're away. But because you won't be distracted by the day-to-day requirements of a job, you'll be able to focus solely on school and may even complete your program faster than someone taking classes part-time. If you choose this path, you'll need to plan ahead and save in advance to cover your lost income and the cost of tuition.

My good friend Angela left her job as an engineer in 2012 to pursue her master's degree full-time in London, England. Her program was 12 months in total. In order to afford the tuition, living costs of London, and forfeited income, Angela had started saving many years earlier and took out a student loan. Upon her return to Canada, Angela secured a job directly related to her studies within two months. For her, focusing solely on school allowed her to finish her program faster and get back to making money.

For many people, however, due to financial or career commitments, leaving a full-time job to pursue an education is not possible; juggling both is the only solution.

I know from first-hand experience how challenging it is to balance work and school. In 2011, I was accepted into a 12-month accelerated master of business administration program. For the sake of my career and financial goals, taking a year off solely to study wasn't a realistic option. Balancing both school and work was.

While continuing to work full-time, I went to classes every other Sunday and Monday and attended six weeks of block classes (classes that run every weekday from eight o'clock in the morning to nine o'clock in the evening), and spent my evenings and weekends buried in books, writing papers, preparing group projects, et cetera. Between work commitments (approximately 40 hours per week) and school commitments (another 40 hours per week) I was absolutely exhausted. To cope, I used any ounce of spare time to sleep, exercise, or enjoy the comfort of my friends and family.

When I look back on it today, I see both the benefits and drawbacks of powering through. I finished the program quickly and with honours, and my career and income didn't stall throughout the process. But I was stressed out and exhausted. There was one morning near the end of my program when I stood staring at my empty refrigerator, in my last pair of clean underwear, pondering what to eat for breakfast. I hadn't shopped for groceries or done laundry in over three weeks. With a little innovation, I melted peanut butter overtop of freezer-burned blueberries. Besides the lacklustre taste of my makeshift breakfast, the worst part was that I was so tired from my advanced-finance all-nighter, I failed to notice my drapes were wide open for all my neighbours to see me in my skivvies. The whole episode sent me into tears.

Fatigue can seriously impact both your work and school performance, so another option is to continue working, but space out your studies over a longer period of time. My other pal, Maria, does just that. She is a young mother of three children, and between working 40 hours a week and shuttling her children between dance lessons and karate practice, she only has time to take one night class each semester as she works to complete her bachelor of arts degree through her local university. Sure, it will take her more than twice as long to complete her degree as it would if she were a full-time student, but having balance between her schooling, work, and personal life is important to her.

Education can also be informal. Take, for example, a young woman who is a fitness trainer. She'd like to broaden her fitness expertise into teaching spin classes. In order to learn how to do this, she doesn't need to take a formal class, she just needs to learn the skills from an expert spin instructor.

Think about where you'd like to take your career in the next 5–10 years. What types of skills and education will you need to make your career goals a reality? If you're not sure, speak to someone who has the type of job you'd like to have. For example, if you'd like to become the site manager of a construction site you currently work on, spend time with the current foreperson. Inquire about education, accreditations, and specific skill sets. Ask for some specific advice on what you could do in terms of education and skills to advance your career. If you don't have those kinds of connections, it can be equally beneficial to review job postings for your dream job. The postings should clearly state the skills, experiences, and education required for the role.

When you have a clear idea of where you want to take your career, you can determine the appropriate level of investment in your own education and skills. Whether you hit the books or not, develop skills that will give you a competitive edge and make you difficult to replace. Competitive skill sets provide leverage during salary negotiations and improve your job security.

GET A MENTOR AND A SPONSOR

Mentorship and sponsorship are very different. A mentoring relationship is one in which a young woman benefits from the advice of someone who is more experienced. Mentorship is very helpful when you're developing a career and learning the ropes in your organization. Let's say you've recently completed the professional requirements for your chemical engineering accreditation. Your mentor could be a more senior chemical engineer at the same organization — or perhaps at a different one — who can offer you a more experienced perspective on how to approach certain technical or "people" problems. More times than not, mentors do not have a direct impact on your salary or promotions. They simply provide guidance and help you, the mentee, expand your professional network.

If you feel that someone within your network would be a good professional mentor, all you need to do is ask whether that person would be willing to make time to mentor you. All it takes is an hour or two every month, quarter, or year. You don't need to spend boatloads of time together to glean helpful information. The mentor-mentee relationship is most effective when the mentee comes prepared to meetings with an organized series of questions and an idea of the type of advice she wishes to receive from the mentor.

A sponsor, on the other hand, is someone within your organization who stands up for you, your career goals, and your salary behind closed doors, advocating for your success with the people in your organization who make decisions about your career. Sponsors are very important individuals who want you to succeed. They are often a former boss or someone you've done work for and seriously impressed along the way. A sponsorship relationship takes time to develop because the sponsor must be convinced and proud of your work; hence, you will have to consistently exceed expectations if your sponsor is going to go to bat for you.

Having a mentor will help you to develop a better work product, which in turn strengthens the sponsorship relationship. And from a strictly financial perspective, having a sponsor will pay off. I recommend developing both mentor and sponsor relationships.

YES, YOU CAN ASK FOR A RAISE

My good friend Cody is the "Raise Master." Every three to six months, he sits down with his boss and negotiates for a higher salary, more time off, a better bonus, and many more perks. What's incredible about this is that Cody is *always* successful in his negotiations. According to him, the key to his negotiations is presenting, in a confident and convincing way, facts that support that he's added value to his organization, and leaving arrogance, whining, and any semblance of a pity party at home. When asked, he said that the first few negotiations were difficult, but they became much easier over time as he learned the best ways to effectively communicate with his boss.

For some strange reason, many young women, myself included, find it very difficult to ask for a raise. I'm not sure if it's that we find it rude to talk about money with our bosses, we feel we don't deserve it, or we don't feel confident we'll be successful in our request. Whatever the inherent reasons are, young women can make more money by following these common-sense approaches to closing the income gap and increasing how much they earn.

Again, in the words of my late grandfather, "If you don't ask, you don't get." According to the Society for Human Resource Management, 33 percent of people — and especially women — say they're freaked out about salary negotiation, so they don't pursue it, yet 80 percent of recruiters and managers are willing to negotiate.

Think you deserve a raise? Get prepared.

Step 1: Know What You're Worth

Before you sit down with your boss to discuss your salary, research comparable salaries for comparable jobs where you live. Use websites like Salary.com, SalaryExpert, Monster, Workopolis, or Payscale. If you belong to an association or alumni group, check whether it has research on salaries and benefits that you can review. It's also important to remember that salary is only one part of a total compensation package. There are other factors to consider, such as benefits, stock options, and retirement plans — all of which are negotiable.

Step 2: Set a Goal

Once you've got your facts straight about comparable salaries, set a realistic goal before you go in for negotiations. Perhaps you want a raise of 3–5 percent, plus stock options. Or you may wish to focus on a number, like $5,000. Whatever the case may be, your goal should reflect market rates, your specific performance, and your plans for the future.

Step 3: Focus on the Future

I had the pleasure of hearing a woman marketing executive speak at an event early in 2013, and she informed the audience of an interesting statistic: men often get raises based on what they say they are going to do, whereas women get raises based on what they've already accomplished. Often, this difference is a result of how men and women present information in salary negotiations.

Could young women be more successful in salary negotiations if they, too, focused on presenting plans for the future along with summarizing successes from the past? Though I don't have any statistics to answer that question, I'd wager a guess that a future-focused discussion during salary negotiations shows initiative and commitment, both of which are highly valuable to any organization. What if it meant an extra $1,000? I believe it's worth a try.

Step 4: Pick the Right Time

Try to avoid barging into your boss's office asking for a raise after your boss has had a hectic day. Wait until you've both got some time to sit down and talk. It's also nice to provide a heads-up about the nature of the discussion so that your boss can prepare — by consulting with an HR adviser as to salary and benefit policies, for example. Another optimal time to discuss a raise is during a regular performance review. Therefore, if you can negotiate to have your performance reviewed more frequently, you create more opportunities to discuss your salary.

Step 5: Communicate Your Value

Don't beg or whine when asking for more money, and avoid making unquantifiable statements or comparisons. Above all else, be professional. Focus the conversation on how valuable your contributions are to the organization and what you plan to do for your company in the future that will create additional value. (Hint: if you want more money, you're probably going to have to take on more responsibility, which could be stimulating for both your career and your paycheque.)

If you feel you are being underpaid, you may also want to present your employer with a competitive offer. If you truly add value to the organization, your boss will want to keep you and may match the competitor's offer. However, be aware that sometimes this strategy can backfire, so if you choose to go down this path, you need to be mentally ready to accept the competitive offer.

Playing the field for competitive job offers requires that you are actively marketing yourself, which means you'll need to have an up-to-date resumé and be prepared to invest time in going through interviews. Late in 2013 I spoke at the 10th Annual Women & Leadership Conference, and the speaker who presented before I did talked almost entirely on the importance of ensuring that women update their resumés and go for at least one interview each year, even if they have no intention of leaving their current organization.

Knowing what you're worth in the job market will help you attain a higher salary, and an up-to-date resumé is a tool that communicates your experience, and is also a form of protection should you lose your job.

Step 6: Enhance Your Personal Brand

Sometimes salary negotiations require a lot of back and forth. This is normal — it's all part of negotiation. Be realistic and patient, and use the time to sharpen your skills. Going forward, do everything you can to enhance your personal brand — what makes you unique compared to your peers — and contribution to the success of your organization. That way you're more marketable in good times and bad.

ASK FOR A PROMOTION

Many women shy away from asking for a promotion. Don't! Go for it! Forget about whether you plan to start a family in a year or hope to take a sabbatical to travel the world. If you're doing a great job and showcasing competence in the field, you deserve a promotion, so tell your boss you want one. Don't opt out because of your personal plans. Until you're ready to actually leave the workplace to have a baby or travel or go back to school, work your tail off and get paid what you deserve. Men do it, so why shouldn't women?

30 SMART WAYS TO PUMP UP YOUR INCOME (AND 10 "STRATEGIES" TO AVOID)

Outside the traditional employment setting, there are smart ways to increase your income, but first, here are some other methods I do not recommend:

1) Start a meth lab or grow weed. Even Walter White eventually ran out of reasons to be in the drug business on *Breaking Bad*, and Nancy Botwin eventually got caught on *Weeds*.

2) Traffic drugs. Do you want to end up in a women's prison just like Piper Chapman in *Orange Is the New Black*? Though the television show and book make prison seem like cakewalk, it's not. You'll never live a normal life again.

3) Tax evasion. Martha Stewart certainly learned her lesson. Before heading to jail for insider trading, she had to pay $220,000 in back taxes and penalties. One way or another, the government will always take their "pound of flesh."

4) Start a dog-fighting club like Michael Vick. Unless it's authorized by World Wrestling Entertainment, most fight clubs, whether animal or human, are illegal — not to mention inhumane.

5) Become an escort. Certainly Joan, who is an office administrator on *Mad Men*, made out okay selling sex for $50,000 and a 5 percent partnership stake in her advertising firm, but that's Hollywood. You could get hurt, and in most places in the world, it's illegal.

6) Deposit empty envelopes in the ATM machine and withdraw your daily allowable limit. Sure, if you're really strapped for cash and only a few days away from payday, this may seem like a good idea — you plan to pay it back, right? Wrong! This is fraud, as is kiting cheques. Cheque kiting works like this: Louisa opens chequing accounts at Bank #1 and Bank #2. She makes an initial $1,000 deposit in Bank #1 and deposits nothing in Bank #2. She then writes a $5,000 cheque on her account at Bank #1 and deposits it in Bank #2. Because it takes three business days to clear a cheque, and Bank #2 doesn't know Louisa has insufficient funds to cover her cheque, Bank #2 immediately gives her credit in her account. Before three business days are up, Louisa writes a $5,000 cheque on her account at Bank #2 and deposits it in Bank #1 to cover her first $5,000 cheque. Bank #1 immediately gives her credit on her account, and Bank #2 clears Louisa's first $5,000 cheque. Louisa continues to write bad cheques to herself, effectively obtaining an illegal $5,000 loan.

7) Sell your prescription drugs. Your prescriptions are for you and you alone. Certainly, some drugs can fetch a pretty penny in the underworld, but it's a seriously illegal and seriously bad idea. You could compromise your own health as well as the health of the unknown user.

8) Send your 10-year-old kid to work illegally at a nearby restaurant. Most countries have well-established labour laws that restrict employers from hiring or putting to work children under a certain age. But this doesn't mean you can't assign chores to your children.

9) Bank on the lottery, or gamble. Your chances of winning the lottery or making it big gambling are super freakin' low. Rather than spend valuable time dreaming about potentially winning big, focus your efforts on legitimate ways to make extra money — your payout is nearly guaranteed.

10) Marry a millionaire. Similar to winning the lottery or making it big gambling, chasing around millionaires and trying to seduce them into marrying you is a waste of time. If they've got half a brain, they'll clue in to the fact that all you're after is their money, and they'll probably tell you to hit the road. If you happen to fall in love with someone who has a lot of money, that's great. But you should discuss the implications your partner's wealth has on you and your personal financial goals.

Because you are a money-savvy young lady, you'll want to pursue legitimate ways to start earning more money. I've pulled together a list of 30 ideas.

1) Start a small business. Did you know that women are the fastest-growing segment of entrepreneurs in North America?[5,6] Women are developing successful businesses in a variety of sectors, from manufacturing to fashion to technology. What's even more awesome about women entrepreneurs is that they create new jobs in the economy at a much faster rate than large corporations.

Do you have a special talent, interest, or hidden skill set? Whether you're into commercial real estate development, science, bodybuilding, writing, soup-making, teaching, painting, plumbing, or interior design, consider turning your hobby into extra income ... but don't quit your day job just yet!

I am a small business owner, and over the past five years I've developed a simple income-building model called the "Core and Petals," which you can use to turn your passion into more income. Envision a daisy flower with its white petals and yellow core — the core is connected to the stem, which is rooted in the ground. The stem and core take in the nutrients that the flower needs to stay alive. Think of the core and stem of the flower as your day job. Your job is necessary for your survival. You collect a salary, which enables you to pay your bills and keep a roof over your head and food on the table. Without income stability, you're not likely to survive.

Now, think of your extracurricular interests as the petals of the flower. Because you have income stability through your day job, it's actually easier, and much less stressful, to start developing your petals as supplemental streams of income. The number one reason entrepreneurs fail at their businesses is they didn't have adequate cash flow. The Core and Petals model actually encourages you to keep working at your day job and generate regular cash flow while simultaneously developing your entrepreneurial ideas in your spare time.

What do you need to get started? Take a brief moment to focus on what you love to do. Then, think of ways to make money off your interests. For example, if you're into fitness training, teach a boot camp. If you're a dermatologist, open your own practice or develop a unique skin care product. Once you've thought of a business idea, start developing a business plan that consists of:

- Vision
- Purpose
- Marketing and communications
- Finances
- Operations
- Technological requirements
- Research and development
- Human Resources
- Leadership

A business plan needs to take into account all the stakeholders and market conditions that are involved in making your business successful, such as customers, social media, environmental impacts, and suppliers. What is the relationship these people and factors have with your revenues, brand, long-term growth potential, et cetera?

Next, research the market for your product or service:

- Demographic
- Size
- Geography
- Consumer trends
- Pricing
- Competition

Then, test your product in the market.

When you're ready, set up a small corporation, partnership, or sole proprietorship using a lawyer or by independently registering the business.

Next, get started! Having a business is loads of work, but the rewards can be truly incredible. Make sure to monitor your progress regularly. When your small business is strong enough to become your primary source of income, it then becomes your core and stem. But it often takes time to develop a sustainable business, and, therefore, it's a good idea to keep your core day job while you put your plans in place.

2) Work extra hours. If you have a job that pays an hourly wage, you could work extra hours and may even receive an increased salary for overtime pay. When I was paying my way through university from ages 17–21, I worked as a teller at the local bank, which was down the street from the school. Whenever I had a slow week at school, I would approach my supervisor about working extra hours. If they were available, I took them. As another example, my brother is an electrician, and if he works past his allotted 40 hours per week, his hourly wage doubles for the additional hours worked. So, when he and his wife were saving up for a down payment, my bro worked as much overtime as he could.

3) Sign up for all government benefits and rebates. Wondering if you qualify for certain tax credits or rebates? Investigate what you're eligible for online or by visiting your local government office. In most jurisdictions there are government benefits for parenting, education, fitness, child care, business scholarships, student exchange programs, employment (unemployment) insurance, tax rebates, health care, housing rebates, medical benefits, and more. Your local government will likely have a benefit finder tool you can use to determine what you qualify for.

4) Sell your possessions. If you've got clutter in your home, organize and get rid of it. The general rule that I use when selling my possessions is if I haven't used or worn the item for 12 months, I sell it. As I've previously mentioned, I'm a huge fan of Kijiji and Craigslist, but you may have a better second-hand website where you can hock your possessions. I used to get sentimental about getting rid of my possessions, but now I just see things like unused books, music, jewellery, clothing, furniture as money-making opportunities.

Sell things you no longer use, and while you're at it, if you see a good deal for something you could turn around and resell for a higher price, do it. Don't forget that you can also sell special services like painting, tutoring, or child care online, too.

5) Sign up for freebie loyalty programs. Chapter 2 summarized the key benefits of belonging to loyalty programs. I'm a huge fan of them, if and when you are a loyal customer. My old friend Charles earns credit card points toward travel when he makes purchases using his Visa. This is very valuable to him because his family is located in the United Kingdom and he lives in Montreal. Without his travel rewards, he would have to pay for his own flights. So, being a member of this loyalty program saves him money.

My bank allows me to use my credit card points toward more than just travel. I can redeem them for contributions to my retirement savings program, gift cards, electronics, luggage, and more. Sometimes, rather than spending money on Christmas presents for my immediate family, I cash in my points for free gifts.

Where do you normally shop? If you frequent the same grocery store, coffee shop, or other retail location, sign up to receive loyalty points. Why pay for your tenth coffee when it can be free? Spending money just to earn points doesn't make sense, but benefiting from your purchases through loyalty rewards does.

6) Take in your recycling. No, this isn't a joke. In many places returning bottles can earn you money, so if you've been sitting on a collection of hefty, smelly bottles, return them to your local bottle depot. You could walk away with a pocket full of dough.

7) Get a roommate. Whether you're single, living with someone, or married, if you've got a spare room, rent it out. You can collect hundreds, if not thousands, of dollars each month in rent. Sure, it will be an adjustment to have someone else living in your place, but with clear house rules, ample respect, and good communication, living with a roommate should be easy.

My friend Trevor, a commercial real estate adviser, once told me that his rule about roommates was as follows: one roommate per $100,000 worth of house. So if your home costs $300,000, that works out to three roommates. I'm not certain that his rule can really apply to all roommate scenarios; in my view, it's more about your personal preferences. If you're an introvert, for example, having more than one roommate might disrupt your Zen. Certainly, when I had roommates, my primary concern was whether I could get along with them and if we had compatible living and working schedules.

8) Rent storage space. If you've got extra shelving in your garage or in your storage unit at your condominium, rent it out. There are plenty of people who will pay to be

able to keep their hockey equipment, bicycles, or books in a safe spot for a specific period of time.

9) Rent your parking spot. Maybe you're car-free or simply have an extra parking spot. Whatever the case, if you're not using it, rent it out. My friend Patrick stores his sports car over the winter in someone's secure parking garage for $1,000. If you've got a spare spot in a densely packed area of your city, you'll fetch an even higher price than if there's plenty of street parking nearby.

10) Sell a crazy story. Maybe you've been involved in a daring rescue mission, or have travelled the world alongside a wannabe–Jacques Cousteau, or perhaps you've invented some wild new way to lose weight. If you've got an interesting story to tell, you may be able to sell it to a book publisher, magazine editor, or television network. Before you make your pitch, you'll need to prepare a clear, well-written, and compelling proposal that'll make media-types salivate at the thought of making your story come to life. If you're successful at securing interest, you'll likely collect revenues in the form of royalty payments. Along the same vein, if you're a creative person, like a songwriter or an artist, look into how to monetize your art.

11) Sell advertising on your website or videos. If you've got a great website or video with serious traffic, advertisers will want a piece of the action. If you're stumped on how to build a great website or make a high-hitting video, consult with your pals who have had success with their own, and interview a few designers. Find out what makes a good site and what attracts quality advertisements — you

don't want to spend time and money building a website and the associated brand only to have cheap and raunchy ads for male escorts flashing across the screen.

12) Participate in university studies and focus groups. Being a guinea pig is a great way to earn extra dough. While in university I signed up for marketing focus groups regularly. For an hour of my time, I would answer questions about product design, advertisements, and more, earning $10 and usually learning something in the process. Some studies, usually conducted at private companies rather than schools, offer significantly more money for your participation.

13) Become a paid secret shopper. Secret shoppers test out customer service and products. Their role is to report on their experiences, generally to the company that owns the store or to organizations that compare various product or service offerings.

14) Become a surrogate mother or "donate" your eggs. Becoming a surrogate mother means giving up approximately 10 months of your life to become pregnant, grow the baby, deliver the baby, and ultimately give the infant to the parents who will raise the child. Having a child is a life-changing experience, and that is what women are compensated for (along with their medical and legal expenses). Certainly, some women offer their services for free, but many others collect fees in the tens of thousands of dollars. You can also "donate" your eggs (technically, you're not allowed to sell them) and receive compensation for them in the thousands of dollars. Both of these options are very personal and

require a great deal of thought before you pursue them because in some way, shape, or form they will affect your life, so don't take the decision lightly.

15) Take advantage of grants, scholarships, and bursaries. Many local governments and foundations offer money for energy conservation, environmental preservation, education, career development, language services, and more. If you're thinking of heading back to school, as I suggested earlier in this chapter, then apply for grants, scholarships, and bursaries. A little bit of research coupled with a compelling application could save you thousands.

16) Review and reduce bank charges. Your bank charges you fees for its services. These fees often get overlooked by many young women because they can be quite small — $1.50 here, $0.50 there, and so on. As you prepare your budget, review your fees carefully. Sometimes you can sign up for a low-monthly-rate fee package that covers off fees associated with ATM withdrawals, deposits, cheques, et cetera. Alternatively, some banks that are predominantly online offer free banking services. But many of these institutions don't have brick-and-mortar buildings you can visit — it's all online.

17) Enter contests. Who knows? You may actually win! Entering free contests simply increases your chances of winning compared to if you don't enter at all. My friend Cody — yes, this is the same friend who is also the "Raise Master" — is the king of contest-winning. No word of a lie — he wins free things at least five or six times a year. His latest win was $600. When he heard the magic cue from his radio station, he called in, answered some silly question about Rihanna and Chris Brown, and won $600 in cold, hard cash. According to him, because so many people just assume they won't win, they don't enter, which increases the odds of winning for people who do take the time to enter. Even if you were to win something that you don't want, you can sell it!

18) Do freelance work. Perhaps you're a writer or researcher. You could freelance your services and make money in the process. Let's say you've got a great idea for a newspaper story on some trendy gossip in your community that readers will gobble up. Pitch the idea to the managing editor of the publication you intend to work with and write the article for a fee.

19) Become a part-time consultant. Let's say you like to party. You could become a part-time party-planning consultant, establish a website advertising your services, target a market like corporations or schools, and sell your consulting services. If you love what you do, you'll have loads of fun in the process.

20) Rent out your place to vacationers. In the summer of 2013, I planned a trip to Spain. Sadly, I ended up not being able to go because I had reconstructive jaw surgery instead. But through the planning process, I made the decision to forgo expensive hotels in exchange for less expensive private vacation rentals. I used the Vacation Rentals By Owner (VRBO) website to browse through my options and found fantastic apartments well-located in both Barcelona and San Sebastian. The cost of a VRBO rental was about half that of a high-end hotel. The experience got me thinking about how

renting out your home, or even a few bedrooms, to vacationers could be a great way to earn extra income. Certainly, this option isn't for everyone, but if you've got a great place that's well-located in a tourist destination, give it a whirl and you could earn hundreds or even thousands of dollars each week. Another popular site for vacation rentals is Airbnb.com.

21) Take a second job. Sometimes earning extra income simply means taking on a second job. To help pay off her credit card debt, my friend Leila got a second job selling clothing at a high-fashion boutique shop in Toronto. It was a great idea at first, but then she ended up spending most of her extra earnings on discounted clothing from the store. The moral of that story is that you should take a second job doing something you enjoy, but that won't cost you more money in the long run — like refereeing, for example.

22) Take a seasonal job. If you love to garden, work in a summer greenhouse on your weekends off. October, November, and December are very busy shopping months, and perhaps you could take on a sales job in the evenings throughout that time. If you like concerts, work as an usher; you'll see the show while managing where people sit in your section.

23) Babysit, pet-sit, or plant-sit. Let your friends and neighbours know that you're available to help them out when they're gone on holidays or at work. My cousin is a teacher, and when she's not working in the summertime, she earns money as a full-time nanny. If you live in a condominium, you could become the honorary

dog-walker for the complex. Your neighbours could drop off their dogs at a certain time, and for $10 per pet, you can take the whole lot for a one-hour stroll.

24) Tutor. Do you have a special skill set others would pay to learn? Become a tutor. You could teach someone a new language or help young students with their math homework.

25) Become a part-time exam administrator. We've all met them before. They're the people who wander up and down the rows of students writing exams. They don't answer questions. They simply inform the students of the rules of test-taking and monitor them to prevent cheating. So long as you're an observant young woman, you'll be successful.

26) Count votes. When I was in high school, we had a municipal election. I applied to count votes in ballot boxes the night of the election. The process took five hours of my time and I was paid $75.

27) Become a model. Do you have a nice face? Hands? Feet? Rear end? Hair? If you've got an attractive feature that you often get compliments on, speak with a modelling agent about showing it off.

28) Sell Mary Kay, Avon, tea, Tupperware, sex toys, spa products, home decorations ... You'll have to drum up your own clients, host parties, take orders, and manage the logistics, but ultimately, the harder you work and better at sales you are, the more money you'll make.

29) Create an app. Do you have a useful idea that you could build an app around? Build and sell it. But before you hire an app developer, test your concept with trusted friends and acquaintances. You don't want to invest in the development of an app that no one will download.

30) Become an odd-job expert. Put a blanket advertisement on Craigslist or Kijiji for odd jobs such as decluttering, house cleaning, window cleaning, cooking, or tour guiding. If someone approaches you with a job that you can't do, simply decline ... but before you hang up, tell them what you're capable of. You never know what people need help doing and what they'll pay for.

IT TAKES TIME

It can take some time to increase your income, which is why adopting a frugal lifestyle *today* is important. You can see the financial impact of frugal living in your bank account immediately, whereas getting a raise or opening a small business can take some time. Be patient as you grow your income and try not to wear yourself out in the process. Working 24/7 will result in you being miserable — and you can't put a price tag on balance and happiness.

CHAPTER 6
You Get What You Save For

SAVING SUCCESS

Angel, a 25-year-old military officer, felt she was in a good financial place. The military had a retirement savings program that both she and the military contributed to, and she was about 14 months away from fully paying off her furniture and car loans. Thanks to the military, her education was paid for and she had no student debt, but, in exchange, Angel had to make a commitment to work with the military long term. Thankfully, she found great satisfaction in her work and was excited about her future.

For a variety of reasons, including having a string of bad landlords and disruptive neighbours, Angel decided it was time to start saving for a home. She was excited at the thought of building equity in her own home and having control over where she lived.

Having never saved for a big-ticket item like a home down-payment before, Angel did Internet research and interviewed two financial advisers on best practices for saving. She set a goal to save a 10-percent down payment for a home that would ultimately cost $225,000 (the amount she could afford), translating into a total of $22,500 in savings. She opened up a safe high-interest savings account earning 2 percent in interest and set up automatic monthly contributions of $1,200 into the account. She knew if she kept up with her savings plan, and earned some interest on her money throughout the process, she'd have enough for her down payment within 19 months.

Since $1,200 a month was a lot of money for Angel, she cut back on small purchases and got rid of her home phone, saving $200 a month; took on a roommate for $600 a month; and started teaching military-style boot camps in her neighbourhood twice a week, earning $400 a month.

Throughout saving her down payment, Angel was tempted, at times, to spend her savings. But she kept focused on her even greater desire to own a home and curbed her temptation. As a reward for her tremendous efforts, she promised herself a trip to a hot Mexican resort when she was done saving. To pay for her adventure to Cozumel, she planned to save the same amount for one additional month, bringing her total time to save to 20 months. With interest, her total savings after 20 months would come to approximately $24,400 ($22,500 for her down payment and $1,900 for her trip).

THE EMOTIONAL REWARD

Angel stuck with her savings plan and not only achieved her goal, she exceeded it! With a little local advertising and word-of-mouth testimonials from attendees, her boot camps became super-popular. When the time came to purchase her home, she was ecstatic because she could also afford to put a little "lipstick" on her new place — fresh paint and new floors. Saving for such a large expense had another added benefit: it forced her to adopt very healthy financial habits, which she was able to translate into her new life as a homeowner.

Being able to afford to purchase a big-ticket item is hugely empowering. I recall the excitement I felt when I had finally scrounged enough money together for my first home, tuition, and a half-decent car. In all three of those instances, I had planned well in advance for the purchases. But when the day came that I paid for each, I was really proud of how I'd handled my money successfully. Yes, I was certainly sad about having to part with my stash of cash, but each item represented a significant milestone in my life. Even today, because I love to travel, I enjoy planning and paying for trips in advance so that when the time comes to hop on the airplane, I'm carefree and don't spend time thinking about how I'm going to pay for my adventure when I get home.

AUTOMATION IS THE KEY TO SAVINGS SUCCESS

Before diving into the details of how to set goals and save for the things that matter to you, I want to let you in on the most powerful savings secret — automation.

Having your bank automatically transfer your savings from your bank account on payday into your chosen savings vehicle (discussed later in this chapter) is critical. Studies have shown that people are far more successful with their savings programs when they aren't personally responsible for making the transactions themselves (i.e., writing a cheque or going online and transferring money between accounts). For some strange reason — I like to call it being human — that plan typically fails because we forget to make the transfer or we spend the amount we had planned to save.

To automate your savings program, all you need is a void cheque and clear instructions for your banker to have the bank withdraw the amount you wish to save on the day you get paid and transfer it directly into your savings plan.

WHAT'S ON YOUR LIST?

Now that you know automation is your best friend when it comes to saving, take a moment to think about the things you want in the next five years. Perhaps you're heading back to school, planning to take a one-year sabbatical to sail around the world, getting married, starting a family, or starting a business. In all these cases, you'll need savings to make your dreams a reality.

Your longer-term goals, like retirement or owning a vacation property, on the other hand, require a different approach from savings. Those are things you invest for, and you'll note that they cost a lot more than items you would typically save for. We'll cover investing in the next chapter, but first, let's look at the best techniques to save money.

In all cases, saving money starts with a SMART goal — Specific, Measurable, Attainable, Realistic, and Timely. An example of a SMART goal is Jenna's: "I want to save $10,000 in the next 24 months, so approximately $420 a month, through automatic bank transfers to a savings account, for a home renovation." Her goal is specific about the amount of money she wants to save and what it will be used for. It is measurable in that she has given herself a 24-month time frame and can track her progress throughout her saving. Jenna has already determined that saving this amount of money is achievable. She applied the Frugal Fundamentals to her personal spending plan and was successful in asking for a raise, so she knows she has the means to achieve her goal. The goal is realistic in that $420 a month boils down to $210 per paycheque, and Jenna plans to have that money taken from her bank account on payday, before she can spend it. (Plus, with a biweekly withdrawal, every two weeks rather than twice per month — 26 withdrawals of $210 each year versus 24 withdrawals — Jenna will have an additional $840 at the end of the 24-month period.) Finally, the goal is timely in that 24 months from now is close enough in the future that she'll still be excited about her home renovation.

On the contrary, Alex's goal isn't SMART: "I want to buy a Chanel bag next year." We don't know how much the handbag costs and when, specifically, Alex wants to bring her little treasure home. We are also left wondering how she plans to save up for the bag and what her motivation is for having an expensive handbag in the first place. For example, will she tuck money away into a savings account or stuff it into jars at home? And, is the bag a personal reward for accomplishing a certain goal or is it just an un-frugal "pick-me-up" purchase? Without a specific time frame in mind, we're also unsure of whether the purchase of the bag will still be relevant for her sometime "next year."

Let's turn Alex's goal into a SMART goal. "I want to buy a Chanel bag next December (10 months away) as a reward to myself for finishing my accounting designation. The bag costs $2,000, and I plan to save $200 a month by withdrawing that amount each month and having my sister hold on to it for safekeeping." Saving that amount is within Alex's resources — she's working full-time and generating extra income by renting out her parking spot. And her goal is timely, as next December is when her accounting program concludes.

SMART goals can be applied to anything — debt reduction, investing, getting a promotion, achieving a certain level of education, building your net worth, raising your self-esteem, meeting a life partner, helping your children grow, or improving your marriage.

The second part of SMART goal-setting is to write down your goals. Young women who write their goals down are far more likely to achieve them than women who don't. This is because the act of writing down your goals brings them into focus!

Why not take an evening to think about your savings goals. Turn off your cell phone, and pour yourself a glass of wine or wrap your hands around a mug of soothing tea. Get your partner to join in, if you have one. Consider your future, and jot down some SMART goals. If you're like me, you may want to parlay this list into an art project. I like to jazz up my goals with some colour and sometimes even magazine cutouts. If you're into Vision Boards, where you visualize where you want your life to be and create a collage out of clippings from articles, pictures, and words that reflect your desired future, just paste your SMART goals onto your art creation.

SAVING LOGISTICS

Both Vision Boards and SMART goals are rooted in the same theory — the more "life," focus, and reminders you can bring to your goals for the future, the more likely it is you'll achieve them.

Once you've got an idea of what you're saving for, you can turn to the logistics. The primary goal when saving, besides achieving your ultimate target amount, is to protect your capital while earning some interest and reducing the temptation to spend. Typically, the best tools to save with are high-interest savings accounts, locked-in low-risk guaranteed investments like guaranteed investment certificates (GICs), certificates of deposit (CDs), or government-backed securities like low-risk money market mutual funds.

Each one of these tools provides security of capital and a reasonable yield (e.g., interest). Because these types of investments are low risk, they tend to earn a lower return when compared to historical market returns. This is why these tools are generally not used for retirement savings. Nonetheless, some interest and returns are better than no interest and returns, which is what you'll earn if you stuff your money under your mattress, in a sock, or in the inserts of your bra.

To effectively reduce the temptation to spend your savings, simply make your accounts non-accessible through your ATM card. GICs and CDs go one step further and will strip you of your earned interest if you withdraw from them prematurely.

Once you know what you're saving for and the right tool to do the job, you'll need to create a plan to make achieving your goal as quick and pain-free as possible. This typically means taking the total amount you want to save and dividing it by the amount of time it will take to get there. So, if you want to save $1,200 in one year, you'll need to save $100 per month. You can break this number down further to the number of paycheques you receive every year. You've probably guessed this already, but the shorter the time frame, the more you'll have to save, so play with this number until it works with you budget.

Let's say you are interested in going back to school to pursue your degree in environmental science, and the program you're interested in taking is in Seattle, Washington. Currently you live in Dallas, Texas, with your husband and two little ones. Your husband can get a job in Seattle, but his salary won't be enough to cover your living expenses. The cost of the program equates to $30,000, and you'll need at least an extra $1,000 per month for living expenses for your family for the duration of the program, which is 24 months. You figure you can offset your living costs by working part-time as a teacher's assistant while you're in school, earning you $500 per month. Your family's moving expenses will be minimal as you'll lean on friends and family to help you pack up and unpack your U-Haul truck in both cities. Thankfully, you and your husband have minimal debts, besides your mortgage, and good jobs, which will allow you to save. The total amount you'll need to save is $42,000 ($30,000 for school and $12,000 for living expenses).

Now, $42,000 is a lot of money for any young woman, especially one with a family. And if you consider the opportunity cost of lost income for leaving your place of work for 24 months, it's an even steeper price tag. But, based on your research, you know that your income-earning ability with your university degree will likely double your salary within five years after graduation. According to your calculations, the long-term benefit of increased income far outweighs the short-term cost of investing in your education.

The earliest the school can admit you is 30 months from today, so you calculate the amount of money you'll need to save each month as approximately $1,400, which is equivalent to $42,000 (the total amount you need to save) divided by 30 months. Fourteen hundred dollars a month is well beyond what you currently have available in your budget, so you become resourceful and rent out your basement for $900 per month, take on some freelance work for $200 per month, and buy underpriced sports equipment on eBay, which you turn around and sell for a higher price, earning you another $100 per month. The remaining amount of money you need to save will come from your regular job and the cutbacks you'll make to your regular monthly spending. Within three months you and your family have adjusted to your new ultra-frugal reality.

Your monthly savings of $1,400 is taken out of your account automatically by the bank on the fifteenth of every month and is transferred to your low-risk guaranteed investment; in your case, you've chosen a CD earning 3.5 percent in interest over the course of the 30 months. The CD offers you protection of your capital, which is your primary concern. When month 30 rolls around, you actually have close to $44,000 in savings due to the amount of interest you have earned on your savings. You use that $2,000 in interest earnings for incidental moving expenses.

Sometimes, young women prefer to save in lump-sum amounts, and that's fine, too. For example, if you receive a tax return or bonus each year, this amount can be put toward savings. Personally, I save both in regular intervals and in lump-sum contributions because that is the nature of my annual income. My regular contributions ensure I never fall behind, while my lump-sum contributions simply help me achieve my goals a little faster.

THE SKINNY ON HIGH-INTEREST SAVINGS ACCOUNTS, GICS, CDS, AND MONEY MARKET MUTUAL FUNDS

High-Interest Savings Accounts

Most financial institutions offer competitive high-interest savings accounts, so scope them out. Sometimes online banks like ING Direct offer an even higher rate and lower fees than a bricks-and-mortar bank due to their low overhead costs, and can pass the savings on to you. Online banks can be accessed via telephone or the Internet. Most savings accounts in North America are insured by either the Canadian Deposit Insurance Corporation (CDIC) in Canada for up to $100,000 or the Federal Deposit Insurance Corporation (FDIC) in the United States for up to $250,000.

Guaranteed Investment Certificates and Certificates of Deposit

A GIC is available in Canada, whereas a CD is available in the United States. Both are low-risk lending investments similar to a savings account. You lend the bank money (the principal), they pay a fixed rate of return (perhaps 4 percent), and then they lend the money to other customers (such as a line of credit at 7 percent). Like a savings account, GICs and CDs are very safe investment vehicles, but they typically pay a higher return than a savings account; however, you lock up your money for a period of time ranging from 30 days to 5 years (and pay a penalty if you cash out early). Tying up your funds in a GIC or CD may not necessarily be a bad thing, since it reduces the temptation to spend.

Longer-term GICs and CDs tend to have higher interest rates because they tie your money up for a longer period of time — the higher rate provides more incentive to the investor. You can purchase GICs and CDs at your financial institution for a lump-sum investment (minimums hover around $500) or in regular intervals through automatic contributions (e.g., weekly or monthly).

Similar to savings accounts, GIC dollars are insured through the CDIC up to $100,000 and CD dollars are insured through the FDIC up to $250,000.

Money Market Mutual Funds

A money market mutual fund is a low-risk investment based on very secure government-backed assets and high-quality, short-term corporate bonds, like treasury bills and commercial paper. A money market mutual fund has no guaranteed return, but typically generates a small, less risky, return. Similar to savings accounts, GICs, and CDs, this product can be purchased at most financial institutions, and you can contribute to it in either lump-sum payments or regular intervals through automatic bank deductions.

Funds saved within a money market mutual fund are not guaranteed by either the CDIC or the FDIC. Therefore, this savings vehicle is considered slightly higher risk.

ARE YOU THERE YET?

Congratulations, you're this far into the book. Now, where do you stand on saving? Take this fun quiz to see your progress.

1) Your employer rewards you $1,000 for doing a great job on a legal case. What would you likely spend the money on?

   a. Spend $400 on some new clothing, save $500 in your investment account, and donate $100 back to the local women's shelter.

   b. Take your two closest friends out for a day of snowboarding and a night in the mountains. The cost of your trip would be $1,000.

   c. Stuff it *all* away in your savings account or in your heart-shaped home safe.

2) You really want a new MacBook Pro with an LCD screen and other accessories. Brand new, it costs nearly $3,000. You:

   a. Borrow the money from your husband, run to the store, and set up your sweet new system. You know you'll have to pay him back soon, but you'll worry later about how you'll do that.

   b. Plan to purchase the system second-hand in a few months using savings from your job. Sure, someone else's fingers have touched the keyboard, but you don't care — you just saved $1,000.

C. Plan to purchase the system in six months, which means you have to start saving $500 a month.

3) You buy a new condominium with your hard-earned money at the age of 31. You've got a reasonable mortgage ($1,200 a month), a great interest rate, and a roommate who pays $400 each month in rent. If you had an extra $300 a month after all your expenses, fun, and necessities were handled, you would:

    a. Lease a car for $300 a month.
    b. Pay down your existing mortgage as fast as possible (you don't like to be in debt).
    C. Use half the money to fix up your condo (adding value) and put the other half toward your mutual fund investments.

4) Because you're recovering from a stint of unemployment resulting from the recent financial crisis of 2008–09, you no longer have savings to pay for the night courses you want to take. You:

    a. Get a second job part-time working 20 hours a week selling flowers, books, and trinkets at the nearby hospital gift shop, and start saving.
    b. Investigate the scholarships and bursaries available to you and take on a few extra hours at work, allowing you to save a little bit more money.
    C. Don't worry at all. You'll take out student loans. Isn't part of each loan forgivable anyway?

5) Your old clunker of a car is about to die. You:

a. Forget about spending money on a car, fuel, insurance, and maintenance when you can take public transit instead.

b. Save up for a quality second-hand car that you buy from a private seller on Craigslist.

c. Head to the local dealership and pick a quality new car.

6) Congratulations! You've passed the bar exam and are now a practising lawyer. When your first paycheque ($4,000) is deposited into your bank account, you:

a. Pay your monthly expenses and transfer the entire remaining balance into your high-interest savings account. What do you need the money for anyhow when you're working 80 hours a week?

b. Celebrate your new job by buying new camping equipment ($1,000), and spend $250 treating your sweetie to something special.

c. Tuck half of it (after expenses) away into your savings account and use the other half to pay back your sister.

7) You work all weekend helping out at your neighbourhood garage sale, and in exchange, your community association pays you $300 in cash. Between happy-hour cocktails at a few neighbours' homes, you lose the cash. You:

a. Have a look for the money, and when your search is unsuccessful, you're bummed, but get over it.

b. Freak out and retrace your steps for three hours.

c. Shrug it off. It's just money — who cares!

8) Knowing that, in the long term, owning a home can be financially rewarding, you set a goal to buy a home

in a few years. This means you'll need to save a down payment. You:

a. Start saving what you can each month and invest the money in a medium-risk mutual fund, knowing that the greater the risk you take on, the greater the potential returns.

b. Set a goal to save $10,000 over the course of the next five years using a GIC, which is secure from market fluctuations but still earns a small guaranteed return.

c. Don't worry about saving up. Your grandfather can lend you the cash when you need it.

Scoring for Questions
(Super Saver = 3, Balanced Saver = 2, Spender = 1)

QUESTION	A	B	C
1	2	1	3
2	1	2	3
3	1	3	2
4	3	2	1
5	3	2	1
6	3	1	2
7	2	3	1
8	2	3	1

If you scored between 8 and 13 points, you need to head back to chapters 1 through 4 because you're still a spender. Read chapter 2 again and adopt the Frugal Fundamentals.

If you scored between 14 and 19 points, you have a balanced approach to spending. Continue to monitor your saving and spending so that your spending doesn't interfere with your savings goals.

If you scored between 20 and 24, you're a super saver. But don't forget that it's still really important to reward yourself from time to time. Otherwise, what is life about, anyway?

Saving a lot of money can seem overwhelming at first. But, with clear goals, good planning, and automatic bank transfers, you can achieve your savings targets much faster than you think.

CHAPTER 7
Looking Forward to the Long Term

YOUR CHOICES TODAY SHAPE YOUR TOMORROW

Thirty-four-year-old Liz was nervously watching her mother approach retirement. Despite working consistently since Liz was a small child, her mother, who'd raised Liz on a small single income, had very little in savings and planned on relying on government support in retirement. Her mother's poor financial situation prompted Liz to start thinking about her own savings habits and what she could do to avoid being under-prepared for retirement.

Take a Seat at the Table

While you are saving for your shorter-term needs, it's important to be contributing to your longer-term goals simultaneously. I know, I know. There are a million priorities for your money, and you probably feel like you're running out of dough by this point in the book, but investing for your future — specifically, for retirement — is *super-duper* important. And, as mentioned in the previous chapter, this requires a different strategy than simply saving for a big-ticket item. Young women must invest for the long term.

Sadly, because of lower earnings, lack of planning, and the financial impact of taking time out of the workforce to raise a family, women are far more likely than men to end up in poverty in retirement. Many experts also claim that women are financially vulnerable in retirement because they don't take control of their financial future, often saving far less than they need to and leaving it up to their spouse to plan — heaven help you if you end up unemployed or divorced at any point in your life, with little savings and limited knowledge on investing.

Late in 2013 a study came out of California that focused on the Millennials (20- and 30-somethings), and it specifically examined the financial preparedness of young women for retirement. Frighteningly, only 17 percent of young women felt they would be able to reach their income-replacement goal, which is essentially the money needed to survive in retirement. This is particularly concerning given that our generation will likely live much longer due to medical advances, will receive much less in corporate and government-sponsored benefits, and may have to overcome higher tax rates, inflation rates, and health care expenses than earlier generations.[1]

If you want a secure financial future, you need to take a seat at the table. You should be present and participating in planning and preparing for your future, whether you like finances or not.

Investing in Your Future

Likely the biggest expense in your future will be retirement. Because today's young women are expected to live until an average age of approximately 83;[2] because some will choose

to live on their own without a partner, forgoing the benefits of dual income; and because the cost of living continues
to increase, we need to save more than previous generations.
Again, banking on the lottery or trying to marry a millionaire
isn't a good plan — the odds are not in our favour.

The great thing is that more young women than ever before
are achieving success in their careers and financially. As a
result, young women are playing a greater role in the financial markets as they allocate their hard-earned dollars toward
long-term investments. When armed with the right investing
knowledge and skills, statistics show that young women can be
highly successful with their investments.

In recent years, studies published by Barclay's Capital, the
University of Colorado, the *Wall Street Journal*, the *Globe and
Mail*, and others have concluded that women's investment portfolios tend, on average, to outperform men's portfolios. The primary reason for women's investment success has much to do with
women's natural predisposition to be more risk-averse than men.[3]

Women naturally gravitate toward Warren Buffett's style of
investing: buy and hold high-quality, less risky assets that will
grow through long-term appreciation and dividends. Savvy
women investors also know that investment markets go up and
down in value depending on the day or overall economic conditions. But overall, historically the markets have increased in
value as a result of factors like growing businesses and innovations. Some volatility shouldn't shake your financial investment
strategy off course, but knowing when to protect money from
market volatility is critical.

Warren Buffett is considered the most successful investor of all time and he believes that the most critical element
of successful investing is to avoid losses. Therefore, a woman's tendency to risk-aversion gives her an innate advantage
when investing. An example of how this plays out in real life is

that when the markets start to tank, like they did in 2008 and 2009, women are more likely than men to pull the pin on their investments, effectively stopping losses earlier and preserving their wealth.

That said, women, like men, are not born successful investors. They have to learn the investment ropes first. Here are five key investment principles young women should follow:

1) Save 10–20 percent of your earnings;

2) Match your risk tolerance with your investment portfolio;

3) Reduce your exposure to risk as you age;

4) Get help;

5) Do your research.

When you follow these steps and start exposing yourself to finances in a bigger way — even if you just read one article about investing each week — you'll position yourself for financial success, which includes being prepared for your expensive future.

STEP 1: FOLLOW THE GOLDEN RULE – INVEST AT LEAST 10 PERCENT OF YOUR EARNINGS

For the reasons I've already mentioned, we need to target investing at least 10 percent of our income, if not more. You'll recall that most wealthy women have scrapped the "golden rule" and advocate investing between 15 and 20 percent of gross earnings.

- The easiest way to step up contributions to your retirement savings plan is, first, to save a percentage, rather than a dollar amount, of your income. This way, as your income increases, so too does your investment contribution. For example, if you net $40,000 a year, 15 percent in savings is $6,000. Let's say you get a raise next year, and your net income becomes $45,000; investing 15 percent of that would be $6,750. If you only invest a specific dollar amount, such as $5,000, each year, your contributions don't grow. Investing a set percentage ensures your savings grow alongside your income.

- The second way to make investing easier is through automatic bank transfers on the day you get paid, just like in the big-ticket-item discussion from the previous chapter. But instead of the money being transferred into a savings account, GIC, CD, or money market mutual fund, it would be invested in assets that are expected to grow more in the long term (to be discussed later in this chapter).

- The third investing strategy is to contribute to your tax-advantaged retirement plan through work. Many employers sponsor retirement savings programs whereby the employer matches a portion of your contribution toward investments for retirement. This is essentially free money, and you should take it! These programs are also automated so that your investment contribution is taken directly off your paycheque, so it never even hits your bank account.

  Let's compare two 35-year-old young women, Roumeet and Gina, who each earn $35,000 per year. Roumeet contributes 8 percent of her earnings to her tax-advantaged retirement plan through work, and her employer matches a portion of her contribution with 4 percent, bringing her total contributions to her retirement savings plan to 12 percent. (She doesn't have to pay taxes on the funds until they are withdrawn in retirement.) If Roumeet starts her retirement savings program today, contributing 12 percent of her earnings each year until retirement at the age of 65, her income grows at 3.5 percent annually, and through the power of compounded interest and reinvested returns she earns a conservative rate of return of 6 percent annually, she will have approximately $520,000 in retirement savings. Wowie! What's truly impressive, though, is that Roumeet contributed only $145,000 of her own money.

Gina, on the other hand, chooses not to invest in her employer's retirement savings plan and instead goes at it alone. To achieve the same results, assuming everything else in the scenario remains the same, Gina has to contribute $217,000 of her own money; that's $72,000 of free money that Gina gave up by not utilizing her employer's savings plan.

	Roumeet	Gina
Personal Contributions	$145,000	$217,000
Employer Contributions	$72,000	$0
Value at Retirement	$520,000	$520,000

You're a smart young woman. If you were Gina and your employer was going to give you $72,000 in free money, wouldn't you take it? Personally, I can think of about 30 ways I could use that money — paying off my mortgage, investing in a business, travelling …

If your employer has a retirement savings program, sign up. It'll only take 30 minutes to fill out the forms, and in most cases you'll even be able to pick your specific investments with the help of an investment adviser who manages your company's retirement savings program.

The 2008–09 financial crisis demonstrated that even company pension plans can be at risk when the markets crash or go sideways. Many employee and retiree pensions of Nortel, for example, were at risk when the company filed for bankruptcy protection in January 2009. Shortly after that, in May 2009, the company announced that its pension plans were only 69 percent funded.

A pension-funding shortfall at your company can put your future pension and benefits in jeopardy. Thankfully, there are agencies that protect some types of plans up to a certain amount, and can intervene in the event of a shortfall. But this doesn't guarantee you'll get all your pension benefits and savings, especially if the fund is severely underfunded. In the event of bankruptcy, pension plan rights fall below bondholder and creditor rights, meaning your pension isn't the top priority in bankruptcy proceedings.

What's also worth keeping in mind is that if you have a company savings program that, for example, invests in the shares of your company, your shares are worth only market value. So if the company's share value is nil due to bankruptcy, so are your shares. Many companies offering a savings program give the option to invest in mutual funds or other investment vehicles as well. If you have the choice, you'll want to pick the investments that are appropriate to your risk tolerance and long-term financial goals.

BUT, don't be scared away from pension plans; indeed, I highly recommend you invest money independently as well as through mandatory government and company pension plans. Do your due diligence to ensure your company's pension program is healthy. That way you won't get sideswiped by an underfunded plan when you have full access to its financial records. If you're still unsure about the health of your company's pension plan after you do some research, consult with a professional financial adviser or lawyer, independent of your organization.

If your employer doesn't have a retirement savings program, or you are self-employed, no worries — you'll just need to open up your own retirement savings plan through a professional investment adviser.

- The fourth, and probably most powerful, way to make investing work for you is to save for retirement in tax-advantaged savings plans. These plans, such as a Registered Retirement Savings Plan (RRSP) or Tax-Free Savings Account (TFSA) in Canada, or 401(k), Individual Retirement Account (IRA), or Roth IRA (named after a Senator) in the United States, are tax-advantaged, meaning at the end of the year your tax bill is reduced by a *significant* percentage of the amount you saved in your retirement savings plan. Employer-sponsored retirement savings plans, like defined benefit or defined contribution pension plans that are registered with the government, are also tax-advantaged.

I don't want to stray too far off the topic of saving for your retirement, but if you're a mother, you also need to know that there are very powerful tax-advantaged savings programs for your child's future education expenses. In Canada, the Registered Education Savings Plan (RESP) is the most popular tool for saving for a child's education. Beyond the tax advantages of the RESP, your funds also benefit from government grants — free money! In the United States, the most common tool is the 529 Plan. Similar to the RESP, the 529 Plan also benefits from state tax advantages, and in some cases matching grants and scholarship opportunities are also available.

Now back to your retirement ... tax-advantaged plans help you save money because they save you money in taxes. Sometimes you realize the savings immediately and pay taxes later on when the funds are withdrawn, whereas other times you pay taxes immediately but save taxes later on. Regardless of when the government takes their tax payment, in all cases tax-advantaged retirement savings plans will save you huge dollars in taxes — a benefit you don't receive if you invest outside of these plans. In that case, you have to pay taxes on all the income and earnings your investments produce.

Before you invest your money in any type of retirement savings plan, ensure that it is tax-advantaged. Only after you've maxed out all your tax-advantaged investment options should you turn to non-registered investment plans.

STEP 2: MATCH YOUR RISK TOLERANCE WITH YOUR INVESTMENT PORTFOLIO

Think of your investments as pieces of furniture in your home, and your home as your portfolio. If you have a mishmash of beanbag chairs, a snazzy leather sofa, and an 85-year-old hand-me-down oak table from your grandmother, all the colours, styles, and tones may not meld together very well. And when it comes time to try to sell your place, you'll fetch a lower price than a similar home in the same area that's well-furnished or even staged.

Investing is similar; you don't want inappropriate investments in your portfolio because you'll lose money. Rather, you want the appropriate mix of assets to suit your needs, risk tolerance, and timeline. Your asset allocation — the specific investments in your portfolio and how much of each — should be driven primarily by your personal goals, need for diversification, risk tolerance, and age. So, for example, a young woman aged 28 with a high risk tolerance could comfortably hold aggressive growth stocks in her portfolio, whereas a young woman aged 38 with a low risk tolerance would be more comfortable with a lower-risk mutual fund.

Since 1970 the annualized rate of return calculated by the S&P 500 Index has been between 10 and 13 percent throughout the long term. Meanwhile, people who hop around from investment to investment, due to inappropriate asset allocation, earn less than 4 percent on their portfolios — barely above the rate of inflation, which has averaged 3.5 percent.

When your investment assets match your needs, you're more likely to make money by staying invested for the long term and in quality assets, just like Warren Buffett. So, don't let the lower recent rates of return derail your long-term investment strategy. A qualified investment adviser can help you to determine your specific investment style and the most appropriate assets for your portfolio.

The Risk-versus-Reward Relationship

Risk is a tricky thing; we strive to mitigate as much risk as possible while still trying to achieve the greatest reward. The risk-versus-reward relationship works like this: The greater the risk you take on, the greater the potential reward. The less risk you take on, the less the potential reward. This relationship can be applied to investments within a portfolio: the riskier the investments, the greater the potential for a higher reward — and for serious losses.

As I've mentioned, studies reveal that many young women are more risk-averse than men. This is neither good nor bad; it just is what it is. Stats show that as long as a woman is invested according to her risk tolerance, she's more likely to stay invested for the long term, like Warren Buffett, rather than hopping around from investment to investment and continually losing money.

Proper asset allocation also means your portfolio is appropriately diversified, so all your eggs aren't in one basket. When you diversify, losing one basket won't be quite so devastating. To allocate your investments properly, it's important to know your investment personality type: conservative, moderate, balanced, growth-oriented, or aggressive.

To help determine your ideal level of risk, take the following fun quiz.

1) When the vice-president of your company comes walking up to you with a grim *you're-in-trouble* look on her face, you:

    a. Listen as she accuses you of something that you didn't do. You don't like confrontation, so you choose not to correct her.

    b. Say, "I'm not exactly sure what the problem is. Can you explain what's happened?" You then listen carefully to what she has to say.

    c. Deny, deny, deny.

2) You've been working full-time for three years and investing approximately 25 percent of your paycheques

into a mutual fund. One day, you go online to check on the performance of your investment account and find that the value of your portfolio has plunged by 10 percent in less than a week. You feel:

    a. Like vomiting.
    b. Neutral — you weren't really paying attention.
    c. A-okay; it happens.

3) Some girlfriends from the good old days of high school have recently treated themselves to Jimmy Choo shoes for their birthdays. Over dinner and wine, the girls razz you about wearing "cheap" pumps. "You can afford to upgrade!" they say. You:

    a. Grab your bag, run across the street to the designer shoe store, quickly pick out a pair of Prada shoes, charge it to your credit card, and strut, well-heeled, back to the restaurant to show off your new kicks to your pals.
    b. Don't respond to your friends and leave the restaurant feeling bad about yourself.
    c. Tell them your shoes are just fine and proceed to explain that you're saving for your future and that Jimmy Choos aren't going to help you build your net worth.

4) Are you willing to hold on to your investments even when their value drops?

    a. No freakin' way! You need to protect your money.
    b. Absolutely. A little volatility never hurt anyone.
    c. Maybe, maybe not. It depends on the reason for the change in value.

5) Your older brother approaches you on your 40th birthday and asks if you want to invest money in his latest business idea — he and a buddy buy beaten-up homes, then renovate and flip the properties. They are offering you a 25-percent annual return if the business makes money. The only issue you see with the deal is that your bro doesn't know how to swing a hammer, let alone renovate a home. You:

a. Give him the dough — a 25-percent return is huge relative to what people have been making in their investments recently.

b. Tell him you'll consider the investment once he's proved he's got the skills to do the job.

c. Let him know you're not interested. The only investments that appeal to you are ones with guaranteed returns.

6) What statement do you most agree with when it comes to investing?

a. I take time to evaluate my risks, and I'll take a risk if the potential return seems worth it.

b. I don't care what return I make, I just want to protect the money I have.

c. I take higher risks because I know I'll get higher returns, even though I also know I can lose more if I'm wrong.

7) You're single and shopping in a store where an attractive and trendy sales assistant works. He approaches you, compliments you on your hip glasses, and asks if you need any help. You:

a. Tell him you're looking for a pair of pants and that you really like his outfit. Hey, if you find some equally trendy clothes, maybe he'll ask for your number!

b. Turn beet red and say, "Thanks, but I can find my own clothes."

c. Say, "Sure, you can help me," whip open the curtains of the change room to show off your half-naked body, and ask for his number when you're leaving.

8) You sit down with a financial adviser to select a long-term investment. You won't need the money for at least 20 years. You're most interested in:

a. Brand-new stocks that have limited performance history but appear to be skyrocketing in value.

b. Investments that have a guaranteed return, even if it's lower than the average market return.

c. A variety of investments that have at least five years of performance history above or at market returns.

9) You are three months away from having to pay tuition. The total cost is $8,000, but you are $4,000 short. You:

a. Explain the situation to your employer and ask for both a raise and extra hours. You save as much as you can in a medium-risk dividend-paying mutual fund, but leave a little fun money for yourself. You also apply for a $1,000 scholarship from your local community association.

b. Take your $4,000 in savings and invest it in a speculative stock. Fingers crossed that you can double your money in three months.

C. Get a second job working evenings and weekends at the local nightclub for the next three months, and save every penny in a high-interest savings account — no more lattes for you!

Scoring for Questions
(High Risk = 3, Medium Risk = 2, Low Risk = 1)

QUESTION	A	B	C
1	1	2	3
2	1	2	3
3	3	1	2
4	1	3	2
5	3	2	1
6	2	1	3
7	2	1	3
8	3	1	2
9	2	3	1

If you scored between 9 and 11 points, you're a **conservative investor** because you are risk-averse. A conservative investor should select the least aggressive investments. Generally speaking, conservative investors have a shorter time frame to invest, as they are typically older, have more assets to protect, and want to generate income. Therefore, the majority of their assets fall into conservative categories, such as fixed-income securities (e.g., government bonds), cash, and some less risky assets like highly conservative equities, money market mutual funds, and treasury bills.

If you scored between 12 and 14 points, you're a **moderate investor**. Moderate investors typically have a medium time frame to invest, are still focused on asset protection, and want their portfolios to generate steady income rather than growth. A moderate investor is comfortable with some risk, but is still considered risk-averse in the broad scheme of things. Therefore, the moderate investor's portfolio tends to be made up of fixed-income securities and some less risky equities, like high-quality blue-chip (non-risky) stocks. Young women who are somewhat risk-averse, but want some growth or who are perhaps looking at protecting their assets for their retirement, fall into this category.

If you scored between 15 and 21 points, you're a **balanced investor**. You'll note that there are more points allocated to this type of investor, and that is because a balanced portfolio of investments is suitable for just about anyone. Balanced investors are looking for long-term growth, but still want security and income. Therefore, their portfolios are balanced between less risky equities and fixed-income securities. Balanced investors want to moderately grow their portfolios by taking the least amount of risk possible given their needs. Balanced investing is essentially a conservative approach to portfolio growth.

If you scored between 22 and 24 points, you're a **growth-oriented investor**. A growth-oriented investor wants significant long-term growth and takes calculated risks for potentially higher rewards. This investor's portfolio is primarily made up of growth-oriented equities (i.e., stocks that are positioned for growth and don't necessarily pay a dividend) that will appreciate in value. Along with potentially higher returns, growth equities tend to have higher risk associated with them. Growth-oriented investors have a long time-frame during which to invest their money and can handle market volatility. Younger investors, typically under 40, like me, tend to fall into this category.

If you scored between 25 and 27 points, you're an **aggressive investor**. Aggressive investors want aggressive long-term growth and are willing to take more risk in order to achieve it. They have the potential to make the most and lose the most of any investment personality. This profile fits individuals who have a lot of time to invest and aren't concerned by short-term volatility. The aggressive investor's portfolio is made up primarily of aggressive high-risk equities (i.e., higher-risk stocks that don't pay a dividend, but have a high potential for growth). More-seasoned (educated) and highly active investors generally fall into this category.

The table below summarizes the types of investments that are compatible with each investor personality.

You'll note that there are mutual, index, and exchange-traded funds for each personality, and that is because there is a broad spectrum of funds that spans from low to high risk.

All financial institutions offer clients far more comprehensive investment-personality questionnaires, which will help you fine-tune the types of investments that will suit your needs. But before you meet with an adviser or open up an online trading account, you need to become familiar with investing basics, like the difference between a stock and a bond, or what mutual, index, and exchange-traded funds are. Step 5 talks about the importance of doing your research before investing. Nearly a third of my previous book, *Rich by 40*, is dedicated to basic investing information.

STEP 3: REDUCE YOUR EXPOSURE TO RISK AS YOU AGE

Again, the risk-versus-reward relationship works like this: the riskier the investments, the greater the potential for a larger reward — and for serious losses.

Younger women have more time to let their investments grow, and they can generally afford to take on greater risks in the hopes of achieving greater returns. But, as they age, life's responsibilities creep into their decision-making. There are more assets to protect, including things like a house, family, or retirement savings. Therefore, risk tolerance tends to decrease as investors age because there's more to protect over less time. Follow the advice of investing experts, and transition your portfolio to less risky investments as you grow older. This will help protect your nest egg.

	Conservative 9–11 points	Moderate 12–14 points	Balanced 15–21 points	Growth-Oriented 22–24 points	Aggressive 25–27 points
Cash	20% portfolio (e.g., high-interest savings, GICs, or CDs)	10% portfolio (e.g., high-interest savings, GICs, or CDs)	5% portfolio (e.g., high-interest savings, GICs, or CDs)	0%	0%
Fixed-Income Securities	low-risk (e.g., government bonds or treasury bills)	moderate-risk (e.g., government bonds, treasury bills, or high-quality corporate bonds)	medium-risk (e.g., government bonds or high-quality corporate bonds)	minimal growth bonds (e.g., corporate bonds)	potential for high-risk bonds (e.g., "junk" bonds)
Equities	low-risk equities (e.g., high-dividend-yield stocks, typically in regulated industries)	moderate-risk equities (e.g., high-dividend-yield stocks, typically in regulated industries)	medium-risk equities (e.g., medium-dividend-yield stocks)	growth equities (e.g., blend of stocks that pay zero dividend and others with a small dividend yield)	aggressive growth equities (e.g., stocks that pay no dividend)
Mutual, Index, or Exchange-Traded Funds	low-risk (e.g., money market mutual fund)	moderate risk (e.g., dividend mutual funds)	medium-risk (e.g., equity mutual funds)	growth (e.g., equity index funds)	aggressive growth (e.g., commodity-based exchange-traded funds)

STEP 4: GET HELP

Even professionals reach out for financial advice. I sit down with my investment adviser at least twice per year to ask questions and review my portfolio and my investment strategy. In between those meetings, my adviser calls me throughout the year when it is time to buy or sell specific investments. We always cross-reference our list of investment selections with the results of my investment personality quiz, and if something looks off track, we discuss and fix it.

Ladies, don't go at investing alone! It is really important to get quality financial advice from a qualified professional. Not sure where to turn for help? Don't fret. Ask your friends, family, and colleagues for referrals to a reputable investment adviser. When you've got a list pulled together, you'll need to make an appointment with each adviser to determine whether you can work together. Ask questions such as:

1) How long have you been in the investment business?

2) What are your qualifications?

3) Do you charge a fee or commission? If so, how much?

4) How many times a year will we consult?

5) What is your philosophy on investing?

6) Do you have successful relationships with other women investors?

7) What do you do when the markets are volatile?

8) Can you put together a sample portfolio that I can

review prior to making a decision on whether to work
with you?

After you've interviewed at least three professionals, you'll
want to pay close attention to how you felt about them. Were
they respectful? Were they confident in their recommendations?
Were they pushy? Did they clearly communicate how they are
compensated? Were they trustworthy? Part of selecting a top
adviser is going with your gut. If an adviser made you leave the
room not feeling confident, that's probably not the right person
to work with. This is just my personal preference, but I only
work with investment advisers who have been in the business
for at least 15 years and have successfully survived at least two
market cycles.

I also recommend you take their business cards home with
you and double-check their credentials against the body that
governs investment advisers where you live. In Canada the primary governing body is the Investment Industry Regulatory
Organization of Canada, and most advisers receive their certifi-
cations through the Canadian Securities Institute. In the United
States investment advisers and brokers are regulated through
a variety of acts administered by the U.S. Securities Exchange
Commission. Many investment advisers hold various designa-
tions, and you should investigate the implications of each.

Fees and commission may make you feel uncomfortable,
but the fact is that most professional investment advice doesn't
come for free. What you'll want to hone in on is how the investment advisers make their money and whether their financial
incentives are aligned with your financial goals. For example,
you don't want to sign up for a fee-based account structure if
your adviser isn't going to actively manage your account —
essentially the adviser would collect a monthly fee and never do
anything for you. On the other hand, overtrading your account

to collect commission won't work, either. Personally, I pay my adviser a commission for managing my money, so he only gets paid when he's working for me, and before he lifts a finger to do a trade, we have a discussion about it and I give permission.

Getting professional advice can save you from making poor financial decisions. Qualified advisers will work with you to help you achieve your financial goals.

STEP 5: DO YOUR RESEARCH

Before you buy or sell any type of investment, you need to have a good base knowledge on investing. Investing with limited information is like gambling; the odds are stacked against you. Some of the biggest mistakes women investors make are selecting investments they don't know anything about, using an investment strategy that doesn't fit their risk level, avoiding research, or taking a stock tip from an unqualified friend.

I'm guilty of it, too. When I was 18, I took a stock tip from my hairdresser. His uncle's friend's cousin passed along the investment advice, claiming this particular technology stock was going to be a huge hit. Kal, my hairdresser, was so hyped up about the stock, it was hard not to drink the Kool-Aid. Once my highlights were finished, I ran home, hopped online, and purchased the stock with nearly all of my savings. Over the next month, I watched both my highlights and investment fade away. The stock was a total dud and I lost the majority of my savings.

I was so frustrated and angry with myself for having been so foolish. If I'd only taken a few more days to read the analyst research on this dog-crap company, I'd have quickly learned that they were on their way to bankruptcy. I felt even worse for Kal because he'd invested his retirement savings, along with his daughter's tuition money, in the company.

The moral of that story is to do your homework and evaluate investment opportunities using factual information.

Before diving into the nitty-gritties on how to become proficient at researching investments, take this fun quiz to gauge where your investment savvy is at.

1) Which statement do you most agree with?

    a. I don't invest and I know diddly-squat about investments.

    b. I invest and I know basic investment information, like the types of investments in my portfolio and where I bought them.

    c. I invest and I know what assets I own and why I have them, and I'm actively involved in managing my portfolio.

2) Your great-aunt Maddie opens an investment account for you. Within it are a few shares in Apple and Google. You:

    a. Call your investment adviser for advice, then flip open your smartphone and research both companies to see which one is expected to grow the most. You buy additional shares in the best company.

    b. Do a little research on each company and decide to hang on to the stocks for the long term.

    c. Sell the shares and withdraw the funds. You need the money to pay for your annual ski pass.

3) You have the choice to invest $1,000 in a growth-oriented energy company that doesn't pay a dividend, or in a large financial institution that does pay a dividend. You:

a. Run screaming for the hills.... Okay, maybe not. But you certainly aren't going to hand over your hard-earned money, because neither option has a guaranteed return.

b. Because you're comfortable with high levels of risk, you select the energy company, knowing that you won't collect a dividend but could potentially see higher returns than with the bank stock.

c. Not being familiar with the concept of dividends, you research it and decide on the bank stock because collecting dividends is essentially collecting free money.

4) You've been investing money through regular automatic bank contributions to a medium-risk stock portfolio each month. The benefit of regular monthly contributions, where you pay an average price per share over the long term, toward an investment plan is known as:

a. Dollar-cost averaging.

b. Investing for the long term.

c. There is no benefit. Timing the market is almost always better.

5) What is not a key benefit of investing early in life:

a. If the market turns sideways, younger investors can react fast because new technology gives them access to research and to online trading platforms.

b. The potential for growth for a younger investor is higher because of the power of compound interest and reinvested returns over a longer time horizon.

c. Younger investors don't have to do as much research on their investments because new smartphone technology helps them pick the best stocks.

6) The key difference between a stock and a bond is:

a. When you buy a stock, you own a piece of the company. When you buy a bond, you lend the company money.

b. You collect interest payments from bonds, whereas all stocks pay dividends.

c. You can't purchase a bond through your broker, only through online trading.

7) Over the long term in North America, the financial markets have gone up and down in response to new innovations, government policies, global commodity prices, et cetera. If you took a snapshot of the performance of the financial markets over the past 50 years, you would see they have:

a. Ultimately increased in value.

b. Decreased in value.

c. Been volatile.

8) If I want to achieve my investing goals throughout my life, one of the most effective strategies is to:

a. Borrow money to invest with.

b. Protect my money when the market gets volatile.

c. Buy investments suited to my investment personality and invest for the long term.

9) One of the most famous investors of all time is:

a. Donald Trump
b. Oprah
c. Warren Buffett

Scoring for Questions
(Savvy Investor = 3, Just Learning = 2, Need Improvement = 1)

QUESTION	A	B	C
1	1	2	3
2	3	2	1
3	1	3	2
4	3	2	1
5	2	3	1
6	3	2	1
7	3	1	2
8	1	2	3
9	2	1	3

If you score between 9 and 15 points, you need to seriously improve your investing knowledge. Start with the basics, like going online to Investopedia.com and pulling up definitions of investment terms, and reading articles for beginners on how to buy a stock or the differences between a mutual fund and an exchange-traded fund. You should also pick a stock — perhaps a brand name you're familiar with, like Nike or Google — and track the performance of the stock over the next few months. You can do this by setting up a mock portfolio on Yahoo Finance. Watch the value go up and down and read information about why it has been changing in value — perhaps the company released negative quarterly financial results, which would have a negative impact on the share price, or maybe the company launched a new product that everyone loves, and the price reacted positively.

If you score between 16 and 21 points, you're doing great but still have a ways to go in improving your investing acumen. Start reading books on investing from investment gurus like Warren Buffett, Benjamin Graham, and Peter Lynch. Current articles on investing can be found in newspapers and websites like the *Wall Street Journal*, the *Globe and Mail*, Morningstar, Investopedia, MSN Money, *Forbes*, Yahoo Finance, and *The Economist*. I would also recommend that you open up a mock trading account and get familiar with picking investments. Obviously, you'll want to have some type of method to picking your investments — a.k.a. a strategy. Perhaps you'll select investments that pay only the highest dividend, or companies poised for near-term growth. Monitor your progress regularly, and if you're finding yourself off track, investigate why. It will help to sit down with an investment adviser to ask questions about successful investment strategies.

If you score between 22 and 27 points, you're well on your way to being a savvy young woman investor. Now it's time to dig deep and start behaving like a pro. If you're not at this point with your investment knowledge, follow the suggestions in the previous two paragraphs and, when you're ready, start digging deep. This means actively monitoring your portfolio, researching your investment choices, and testing your investment theories out on a qualified investment adviser before confirming any trades.

DIGGING DEEP

On its own, the price of a stock or fund means nothing, but when you compare price, earnings, debt, industry, and other factors against other companies or funds in the same peer group (sector, size, and line of business), you get a better picture of what the company or fund is all about.

If a particular stock has caught your eye, start by visiting *www.sedar.com*, which is provided by the Canadian Securities Administrators, or *www.sec.gov/edgar.shtml*, which is provided by the U.S. Securities Exchange Commission. On either site you can pull up any public company's financial statements, annual reports, quarterly results, and other material documents. If you're interested in evaluating a mutual, index, or exchange-traded fund, check out Globe Investor's Fund Filter or the information on fund performance on Morningstar.

News reports and analyst research are highly informative and can be accessed by doing a basic search on your favourite search engine.

Investment analysts prepare informative reports on various companies and funds, covering line of business, competitive assessment of the business, historical financials, share price performance, earnings per share, capital-expenditure plans, debt position, and growth rates. Analysts also predict the future of each of these factors. Analysts wrap up their research by setting a target price for the stock or fund and providing an opinion on whether investors should buy, hold, or sell the stock or fund. If you have a brokerage account (discount or not) or an investment adviser, you'll have access to research produced by the firm where your account resides.

Analyst research is supposed to be an independent assessment of a company or fund, but because institutions can sometimes be closely tied to the companies the research analysts cover, "independent" assessments can be somewhat influenced by existing relationships. Therefore, gather research from a few different sources to get an objective opinion. Besides reading research reports provided to me by my investment adviser, my go-to websites for investment research are:

- Investopedia

- Globe Investor

- Forbes

- Morningstar

- Yahoo Finance

- SEDAR

- EDGAR

- TMX Group

- New York Stock Exchange

Knowing where to go to get good financial information and investment research will help you become a smarter and more successful investor, whether you're into stocks, bonds, mutual funds, exchange-traded funds, or index funds.

Doing research up front will help you avoid losing money by selecting quality investments suited to your investment profile. Peter Lynch, a highly successful investor like Warren Buffett, has been quoted as saying, "Whoever turns over the most rocks wins." Generally, he is, of course, referring to making money in investing. If you ever get the chance to read some of his work, you'll know that what he's actually referring to is doing your homework. Investors who do their homework are far more likely to make a better investment decision than those who don't. That's simply due to the fact that informed investors have more knowledge to make quality investment decisions.

If only I'd taken Peter Lynch's advice when my hairdresser made his stock suggestion. I could have saved myself a lot of money … and embarrassment!

IMPROVING YOUR ODDS

Sometimes, I daydream about what it would be like to win the lottery. I can only imagine how $1 million could change my life and the lives of those around me. I could stop working so hard to save and invest my money. Wow! That sure would be nice.

But the odds are stacked against every lotto ticket purchaser — one in tens of millions of people win. So why play? Many people who do are drawn to the game because they believed that if their "what if" daydream actually comes true, the financial reward could be greater than what a lifetime of investing could produce. But that isn't necessarily true.

You have the ability to improve your financial odds thousands of times over simply by sticking with tried-and-true investing principles.

Rather than purchasing $25 a week in lotto tickets, invest that money in a tax-advantaged retirement savings plan. If you started contributing $25 a week at age 25, retired at 65, and earned 8 percent annually on your portfolio over the course of 40 years, you'd have approximately $350,000 in retirement savings. If you doubled that weekly amount, under the same scenario it would total $700,000 by retirement (run your savings scenario with the free retirement savings calculator at *www.getsmarterabout money.com*).

For most young women, however, winning the lottery will never happen, so don't bank on it as your retirement savings plan!

If, and only if, you're already making maximum contributions to your tax advantaged retirement savings programs, then playing the lottery from time to time isn't the end of the world.

As with most things in life though, moderation is key. But don't play the lotto at the expense of paying your heating bill or making contributions to your retirement savings.

CHAPTER 8
To Save and Protect

PROTECTING WHAT YOU'VE WORKED SO HARD TO EARN

Imagine following all the advice in this book and not doing anything to protect your money. You could lose everything you've worked so hard for. In the following chapter, you'll make the connection about how your money is closely linked to your intimate relationships, and how some of the best financial and personal protection you can give yourself is to invite people into your life who share similar monetary values. Before moving on to the next chapter on relationships, though, let's look at simple things any young woman can do to protect her money.

SAVING FOR AN EMERGENCY

In the fall of 2011, I went hiking in beautiful St. John's, Newfoundland. I'd been working at a conference all day, and after the last speaker session, I decided to head out for some fresh air. While gawking at the ocean, I neglected to watch where my feet were headed. I missed my step and fell flat on my face.

My fall was epic, resulting in scrapes and bruises, whiplash, a minor concussion, and a cracked and displaced jaw.

For two and a half years after my accident, I sought treatment from a slew of doctors, dentists, physiotherapists, chiropractors, massage therapists, orthodontists, and surgeons. Ultimately, I had to have reconstructive jaw surgery in the summer of 2013 to fix my broken jaw. My total expenses from this incident amounted to approximately $40,000. Unfortunately, like many young women, my medical insurance was limited, covering only a few thousand dollars. So, somewhat begrudgingly, I dug into my emergency funds to pay all my medical bills. *And* I'm glad I did. Health is so important!

My injury was a classic example of why it is important to have emergency funds. You never know when or if you'll experience an emergency with your home, health, or employment, and in many cases insurance only covers a portion of these expenses. Experts recommend that every household have three months of salary tucked away in case of an emergency. This is a lot of money!

However, you can see how important these funds become when an emergency rolls around. To make the process of saving less painful, I suggest you build this fund over time through automatic contributions to a savings plan that earns interest. Start by setting aside 3–5 percent of your income; then increase it to 6 or 7 percent when you're ready. It will take a few years to accumulate enough for an emergency fund, but once you've achieved your savings goal, you can stop contributing.

Again, keep the money somewhat accessible, but removed from your day-to-day spending as outlined in chapter 6.

INSURANCE

I know it's not pleasant to think about illness, disease, death, disability, floods, fires, accidents, and other awful events, but catastrophes can happen, and you need to be equipped with the right insurance to get you through difficult times. Insurance is entirely about protecting yourself. The last thing you need to worry about if your spouse dies or you get into a major car accident is money problems. Trust me — it's worth getting your coverage properly organized now so you can rest easy in the event something terrible happens to you or your family.

The trick with insurance is to insure for the major things and people in your life, such as your house, vehicle, loans (such as your mortgage), future earnings, and life. All you have to do is picture the worst catastrophes that could happen to you, and that should help you to determine what the most important coverage should be for you. So, for example, if you got into an accident at work and could never work again, you'd want your income to be protected with disability insurance. Or if you owned a home and it burned down, you'd want home insurance that covers fire damage. When I had reconstructive jaw surgery and was unable to work for two months, I was very thankful to have short-term disability insurance. It protected my income. Another way to think about what to insure is if your survival depends on it, you should insure it.

Avoid insuring for petty things — it's generally a ridiculous waste of money. Don't buy extended warranties on computers, cars, repairs, and maintenance programs. Avoid pet and child life insurance (adult life and disability coverage is often suffi- cient for a family, but always ensure you have adequate medical insurance for you and your family). Unless you're sending something astronomically valuable in the mail (you should probably avoid doing this, anyway), don't insure your packages. Avoid gimmicks like identity theft, bicycle, eyewear, or extended travel cancellation insurance. Think of it this way — if the loss of something isn't going to cause you financial catastrophe (bankruptcy), don't buy insurance for it.

When you avoid insuring for the small things, it allows you to focus on insuring for larger, more important things like your life or disability. What you don't want to have happen is to be paying insurance premiums on your mail package when you don't have adequate medical insurance.

Work with an insurance broker in your community to understand your needs and select the best products for your situation. If the broker tries pressuring you into buying petty insurance, fire her! Similar to your investment adviser, only work with someone who is reputable and has many years of experience.

WHY A WILL?

Thinking about death is unpleasant and depressing, but it can't be avoided — you need to plan for the inevitable. Having your financial house in order means being organized so that your loved ones can navigate through difficult times as easily as possible. Without a will, your family, spouse, or partner is left working with the government to direct assets.

A will is a key component of estate planning — how you want your assets managed when you die — that ensures your wishes will be honoured. It is a legal document specifying what you'd like done with your assets and other belongings after you die.

Estate planning experts recommend you should have a will prepared if you're over 21 years old (this is because you're likely starting to work and accumulate assets and liabilities), are married or living with a partner, have dependants or children (biological or adopted), or have acquired assets such as a home or liabilities such as a mortgage.

A will protects your estate from unnecessary taxation and specifies how your property, such as a house or investments, is to be distributed when you pass away. It's an opportunity to designate the people or organizations you want to receive your property. It also allows you to specify who you would like to care for your children should their other parent also be unable to care for them. Lastly, you should select an executor of the estate to carry out the wishes of your will.

Should a medical situation arise, a will, and more specifically a personal directive, identifies who can make decisions about your health if you are not able to.

To draw up a will, you can see a lawyer or a paralegal. You can also do it yourself, but I don't recommend this option. If, however, you decide to draw up a will on your own, use a high-quality software program. Once it's prepared, I'd recommend taking it to a lawyer or paralegal for review. Seeing as you'll have to get a professional opinion on it anyway, it may save you money to just draw one up with a professional in the first place. If the document is satisfactory, it should be signed and notarized (you traditionally need two signatures — do not have a beneficiary sign). Once signed, ensure your executor and appointed guardian for your children have a copy. Keep the original copy in a safe place.

Along with your will should be an updated list of all your assets and liabilities. As part of your review, if you haven't already done so, assign beneficiaries to your registered investment funds and pension plans to avoid unnecessary taxes. All debts must be paid after your death, and what's left over, minus fees, is distributed to your beneficiaries. Therefore, administratively, it's much easier for your executor to honour your wishes if you have provided a clear view of the situation.

Review your will and estate plan at least every one to two years, and update them as your personal situation changes — through marriage, children, finances, divorce, death, or a move, or if you want to change your beneficiaries, guardian, or executor.

AVOID EXPOSURE TO FRAUD

In 2012, I was travelling in France for a vacation. In Paris I used the hotel Wi-Fi to access my online banking and pay a bill. While I was online, my Visa number was electronically swiped, and the following day my credit card was cut off because the security department at Visa flagged a number of unusual transactions on my account.

I consider myself a financially savvy young lady, but despite the precautions I'd taken to protect my private information, I never thought to ask the hotel about their Wi-Fi security. Thankfully, Visa caught the fraudsters and put a stop to their spending spree, but I learned a valuable lesson — I need to better protect my money.

Frugal women adopt tried-and-true anti-fraud best practices, and you should, too.

Use secure wireless networks when you access the Internet. I could have potentially prevented my fraud experience by avoiding signing into my accounts while on an unfamiliar server. I also made the mistake of not logging off my accounts immediately when I was finished.

When I got in touch with Visa, the very first thing I had to do was reset my passwords and make them more complex. As a best practice, change your passwords regularly (every few months). Ensure the password is difficult for fraudsters to guess and contains a combination of numbers and letters.

When surfing the Internet or social networking, limit the amount of information you disclose. Whether through email or on the phone, never give out your address, phone number, or banking information to an unfamiliar source.

If you've used a public computer, clear the browsing history when you leave so none of your personal details remain.

Filter out bogus emails and phone calls. If you receive unsolicited email requests for information or even to click on an unfamiliar link, verify the message and sender using a third party unrelated to the message. If you don't recognize a phone number, don't pick up. Legitimate people will leave a message.

When shopping online, ensure the payment website is secure. If you're not sure it is, call the company that makes the product directly and talk to their customer service manager.

Ensure your computer's operating system is fully updated and that you have a robust security system that blocks pop-ups and includes a personal firewall as well as anti-spam, anti-virus, and anti-spyware features.

Cover your hands when entering your PIN, and keep close watch on your bank and credit accounts to ensure there are no funny transactions.

If you travel, call your bank and credit card company to let them know where you are going and for how long. This allows them to detect unusual transactions, just like they did for me while I was in France.

Check your credit score at least once a year to see that there are no errors or items you don't recognize. If you discover a problem, contact the credit bureau immediately, and bring in law enforcement if you believe you've been defrauded.

Last, get a home security system and safe to lock up valuable documents, jewellery, and more. Though it won't prevent break-ins or theft from happening, both will slow down an intruder.

I don't believe in anti-fraud insurance. Nope. I think it's a waste of money because it can only help you after the fact. Hands down, the best way to protect against fraud is to prevent it from happening in the first place using common sense and adopting anti-fraud best practices — just like wealthy women do.

Ultimately, keeping what you've worked so hard to earn is entirely up to you. Be practical and always take steps to protect yourself.

CHAPTER 9
Relationships and Money — Don't Be a Dope

PICTURE-PERFECT TO BROKEN

Hema, a 37-year-old doctor, recently divorced her husband, Franklin, a 40-year-old lawyer, in a lengthy legal battle. Throughout her marriage, because Hema never cared much about money, she paid very little attention to the household finances. Her main concerns were to drive a nice car (a BMW sport utility), live in a big home in an upscale neighbourhood, and send their daughter to private school. But because Hema turned a blind eye to her bank account, unbeknownst to her, she fell victim to financial abuse.

Financial abuse comes in many forms — stealing, not consulting with the other partner on large purchases or financial decisions, withholding funds, excessive gambling, depriving one partner access to funds, lying about the status of the household finances, et cetera. In Hema's case, without her knowing, Franklin spent their life savings, including taking out the equity in their home through their pre-existing home equity line of credit, to buy into a high-risk speculative property development project. When the property management company went belly up, Franklin lost the entire investment. He tried to keep the ordeal a secret. But the cover-up surfaced when Hema's credit card was declined and she started to probe for answers.

Feeling utterly betrayed by her husband both financially and personally, Hema filed for divorce. In her mind, there was nothing that could fix the trust that Franklin had broken. If only she'd been more involved in the day-to-day financial affairs, she probably could have prevented this catastrophe. Thus, she also blamed herself.

When the divorce proceedings concluded, Hema was left with $85,000 in consumer loans and no assets.

THE RELATIONSHIP CONNECTION TO MONEY

Considering that money issues are the leading cause of separation and divorce in North America, in the vast majority of cases, couples don't talk about money nearly enough. Sure, money can't be the centre of attention in your life, but downgrading the importance of financial compatibility below that of travelling, clothes, cars, careers, rings, weddings, houses, and children is utterly dangerous.

Your financial compatibility with your partner is as important as personal compatibility because financial choices are, in many ways, a reflection of a person's value system. If, for example, one partner wants to save for the couple's future, but the other partner spends savings on clothes, trips, or gambling, the couple's priorities aren't aligned, and financial distress will result.

On the flip side, when couples are financially aligned, they truly can accomplish their goals and have a lot of fun along the way. My brother and sister-in-law, for example, have regular weekly discussions about their finances and plans for the future. Because together they've created a plan for themselves, which includes travel, paying off their mortgage, and, eventually, a family, they work jointly toward their future — one that they created and are excited about.

The difference between Franklin and Hema and my brother and sister-in-law is that Franklin and Hema were not headed in the same financial direction. And you know what happens in a game of tug-of-war — no one goes anywhere. The relationship doesn't grow and dreams are never realized.

According to multiple recent surveys focused on uncovering why women are so financially vulnerable nearing retirement, many women don't own their financial future, often allowing their partner to steer their financial ship — just like Hema. Sure, women often make the bulk of the spending decisions in the household, but buying groceries or a new car has *zero* impact on how financially secure a woman will be in retirement.

By this point in the book, you're well on your way to becoming a money-savvy young woman all on your own. Don't jeopardize your incredible progress by neglecting the link between your relationships and money, and don't let someone else determine your financial fate. Again, you need to take a seat at the table that is your future!

YOU DESERVE AN AWESOME FUTURE

Who you choose to bring into your life matters. How they treat you matters. How they handle their money matters. How hard they work at their career matters. All of these things will affect your future.

Recall from the introductory chapter the three pillars that support your future — personal, financial, and professional. The pillar of your personal life is as important as the financial and professional pillars. Because your finances and relationships are interdependent, any weakness in one will compromise the other, which will weaken your career in the process, ultimately destabilizing your future. It's important to strike a balance between the three and strengthen the whole lot throughout your life; only then will your dreams for the future come to fruition.

If you want to create a great future for yourself, surround yourself with awesome people who treat you with respect, challenge your thinking, help you shoot for the moon, and encourage you both financially and professionally. Sometimes, these people are different from you, and that's okay. In fact, differences can add zest to life. But, fundamentally, it's critical that you and your intimate partner are headed in the same direction and are working toward common dreams.

Ladies, you deserve an awesome future — one that inspires you every day to be your best! Take control of your future and strengthen the link between your relationships and finances.

DON'T BE A FINANCIAL DOUGH HEAD — AND DON'T DATE ONE

Choosing what's best for you and your future begins with you! I had the pleasure of hearing Meg Jay, a clinical psychologist specializing in 20- and 30-somethings, speak at a conference in October 2013. Among many fantastic things she said throughout her speech was one key message: the best time for a woman to work on her marriage is before she gets married. What she was referring to was the importance of investing in ourselves — career, personal development, and finances — before walking down the aisle. This personal work strengthens a young woman so that she can make better choices for her future, including one of the most important decisions — who to marry and/or become a life partner with. You must check out Meg Jay's 2013 TED Talk to fully understand her perspective on young women at this critical stage in life.

Someday, your financial situation will impact your life partner's future, and vice versa. And after reading this book and investing time in improving your personal, professional, and financial pillars, let's face it: you're not going to want to date or form a household with a financial dope. On the flip side, if you choose to carry on being an overzealous, credit-card-carrying shopaholic with bucketloads of debt, ultimately distracting you from making healthy career and personal choices, you're likely to scare off financially savvy, emotionally healthy, and respectful suitors.

Irresponsible money management is a huge irritant for people who are dating; one person might feel pressured into paying for everything, or sense the other partner isn't committed to a long-term financial plan. Bad financial habits such as debt and poor spending patterns limit new couples as they plan trips, enjoy meals out, consider re-arranging living situations, and so on. This results in resentment, not butterflies.

It's ultra-sexy to date someone who doesn't tow monetary baggage and whose financial house is in order.

Adopting best practices from this book will help you take care of you — for your financial benefit, not anyone else's. In the process though, you'll certainly increase your marketability in the dating world.

So get organized to rid yourself of debt. Cut up all but one credit card and make a list of who you owe money to, and how much. Negotiate interest rates and consolidate expensive credit card balances. Trade in your $3 Italian soda for a free glass of water so you can pay a little extra on the debt with the highest interest rate. If you're severely overextended with your house or car, downsize both. If you can't keep up with payments, see a credit counsellor.

If overspending is your problem, fix it. Remove all temptations to spend. Unsubscribe from shopping websites or online coupons. Draw up a budget and stick to it. Hide credit cards by burying them in the backyard. Don't go to malls, plazas, and other shopping venues.

Plan a bright future by starting to save and invest using tax-advantaged retirement plans. Sign up for your company's retirement savings plan and contribute the maximum amount. They might even give you free money. If you're self-employed, the tax advantages associated with your registered retirement savings are huge, but you'll have to set up your own plan through a qualified financial institution.

I don't suggest steering clear of dating while you're reducing debt and growing assets. Rather, put together a responsible money-management plan that shows you care about your future. You'll feel much better about yourself, which means you can be more yourself when you're in dating mode.

If the other person is the financial problem, you'll want to discuss ways to improve the situation … or just give your sweetheart this book.

Now, I know that talking about money has historically been considered a social faux pas, but these days it's critical. No, you don't need to scare off your honey with all your money talk. But you do need to start chatting about what's important to you.

Before you walk down the aisle or live together, talk about your views on money: where the views have originated from (e.g., parents or friends), spending versus saving, frugality, debt, buying property, charitable giving, and your career path and the income that goes with it. Ask each other about your hopes and dreams for the future — this is the fun part. Then you can work back from there. So, if you and your honey want to own a sailboat and live on the West Coast, talk about how you can make that a reality.

I'd take it one step further and discuss whether a marriage or common-law contract, like a prenuptial agreement, is appropriate for your financial situation should you decide to move the relationship forward. These contracts simply define how you and your partner want your finances handled should the relationship break down in the future. Though some people are adamantly opposed to these agreements, it's important to consider the alternative, which is allowing the courts to decide the fate of your finances in separation and divorce proceedings. These types of contracts are personal, and the couple must decide what's right for them. Rest assured, many relationships remain very healthy even with marriage and common-law contracts.

At the core of these conversations, what you should try to discover is if your views are fundamentally aligned. If not, do not pass Go! Sweeping financial incompatibility under the rug won't solve anything. It will resurface later.

DOES COMMUNICATION SOLVE EVERYTHING?

Picture this: You and your partner have formed a permanent household and have never spoken about money until the day you apply for a mortgage and are declined. You find out that your sweetheart declared bankruptcy three years before meeting you. Because it was years ago, your partner felt it wasn't a material piece of information to share, and didn't realize it would impact future borrowing ability. You feel frustrated and are kicking yourself for not having "The Money Talk" before you moved in together.

Besides infidelity, the fastest way to end a relationship is to avoid communicating about money. Again, monetary choices reflect a person's values, like trust or greed, and relationships can survive only if values are aligned.

Stop your relationship from hitting the rocks and start talking about money. Learn about your partner's financial philosophy and work to align goals. If you're like most couples, avoiding heated money conversations like the plague, wipe the sweat off your palms and breathe.

Start by setting aside an hour each week with your partner. Grab a coffee, get comfy, and turn off your phone. Set some ground rules about how to behave, such as avoiding finger pointing, sticking to the facts, and focusing on solutions. If you press each other's "hot buttons," back off, cool down, find out why, and keep the conversation respectful. There's no room for shouting in a healthy money conversation.

Your first discussion should be about coming face to face with your shared financial reality. Lay all your cards out on the table (both figuratively and literally) and perform a simple audit of your money situation. Figure out what you're both bringing home, what you're spending, how you're spending it, and what your situations are like in terms of debt, savings, and investing. Once you've had a glimpse of the total picture, you'll need to discuss what's working and what's not based on what you see on paper. Sometimes it helps to jot down these pros and cons.

From there, over the course of the next few money conversations, move the discussion into areas of behaviour and attitudes. If your partner is a cheapskate and it bothers you, bring it up, but don't say *cheapskate*; after all, you're not likely to get far in this discussion — or relationship — with name-calling and judgmental comments!

Gain an understanding of the origin of your partner's financial views. Most 20-to-40-somethings have received little professional advice and limited financial education, and their parents have had the greatest monetary influence, both for good and bad.[1] Chat about what was learned at home or school and what influence it's had.

Next, sharpen your money savvy together by reading and discussing financial books like *Smart Couples Finish Rich*, *Rich by 40*, *The Millionaire Next Door*, and *The Wealthy Barber*. Then, cozy up to your laptop and visit personal finance sites like Yahoo Finance and Investopedia. The idea here is jointly improving your financial savvy so that, in the next phase of conversations, you are armed with the knowledge and skills to make better financial decisions.

Simultaneously, while you're sharpening your financial acumen, you need to get a full list of the financial "chores" in your household. Each week or month, swap who is responsible for paying the bills online, negotiating interest rates, monitoring the budget, or collecting receipts to track your spending. Do not abuse the chore-swapping by making unilateral decisions about your finances. It's simply financially prudent to swap your roles from time to time so that both partners are aware of the total financial position of the household. Though you may not like to deal with certain financial matters, it's irresponsible to ignore them.

As you grow, migrate the conversation to common ground, which is why you got together in the first place. Discuss dreams for the future — buying a home, changing careers, raising children, or travelling. What's the price tag? Envision a typical day in your life next month, next year, and a decade from now. Come to agreement on lifestyle priorities: Is your Mercedes lease payment more important than affording maternity leave or paying off your mortgage faster? Clear priorities translate into realistic goals, which should ultimately support your dreams. Dreaming together will also help reignite your passions for each other.

At the root of your goal-setting discussions, plan to build net worth through debt reduction and asset growth. Your nest egg is what will fund your future. Talk with your partner about a debt-free life, saving for short-term goals like a down payment, and investing for long-term goals like retirement. Consider the importance of having emergency funds and insurance. Discuss investing techniques like automatic contributions to retirement savings plans.

When you and your partner have a clear idea of your financial goals, it's time to sit down with a financial adviser. Interview at least three people and select the one who is most aligned with your goals and philosophies. Financial planning advice from a professional, like a Certified Financial Planner (CFP), helps couples avoid arguments and form a holistic plan.

RELATIONSHIP ROADBLOCKS

Overspending causes severe arguments and stems from unclear financial boundaries. The saver, for example, may feel her financial security is being jeopardized by her partner's shoe fetish. Tell your partner how debt impacts you emotionally and financially. If you're angry about how you got into debt, air your grievances. Agree on what's worth going into debt for in the future, and how you plan to reduce it now.

Dr. Thomas Stanley, author of *Stop Acting Rich*, studied lifestyle choices of real millionaires (not those pretending) and found they're ultra-frugal, driving $30,000 Toyotas, living in homes valued at less than $300,000, and serving $10 to $20 bottles of wine.[2] If you're living beyond your means and going into debt, change your behaviours. Turn the tables on the problem and play a new game: keep what you earn. Tackle the problem together — downsize your home, trade in the Benz for a Honda, put your kids in public school instead of private school. Set up a budget to control spending, get rid of expensive consumer debt first, and going forward, only incur good debt in moderation for assets, like a home.

Don't hide debt from your partner. Re-read the strategies to get rid of debt as quickly and efficiently as possible in chapter 4.

THE WINNING FORMULA — TEAMWORK AND A PLAN

Marriage counsellors agree: teamwork and financial boundaries are critical when planning your future with someone. Remember, though you may not like to deal with financial matters, it's irresponsible to ignore them. Consider the task of checking up on your finances like regular maintenance on your car. If you care for your vehicle, it will run smoothly and longer than if you neglect it. You don't want to find yourself in a bad financial position you weren't aware you were creating. Again, that is why financial chores like paying bills and buying stocks should be shared.

As a team, sticking to an agreed-upon budget allows you to spend less time worrying about money and more time on your relationship. It's a tool to track income and expenses, set boundaries, and support your financial goals. Rather than viewing your budget as restrictive, incorporate affordable fun. Review chapter 3 to determine best practices for budgeting. If you're short each month, cut back. If you've got a surplus, congratulations; you need to save more.

Preparing a budget can be infuriating if one partner is an overspender. Therefore, you'll need to find a way to hold each other accountable while avoiding finger-pointing and sticking to tried-and-true budget principles — spend less than you make, and before you pay bills, save at least 10 percent for your future.

Wondering if you can plan your financial future without having joint accounts? So long as you work together to achieve your goals as a team, your account structure is a non-issue. The benefits of combining accounts, loans, and assets are: fewer accounts to monitor, easy sharing, transparency (helps with budgeting, taxes, and communication), and reduced banking fees. But sometimes when couples pool money, it creates the perception they're flush with cash, which triggers overspending.

Regardless of your structure, be aware that from a legal perspective, unless you have a legal agreement stating otherwise, all assets and liabilities accumulated throughout your union are shared equally. Furthermore, your future will be impacted by your partner's cashflow limitations, attitudes, and behaviours toward money and potential to take on more debt.

The last part of the winning formula when it comes to relationships and money is to develop a written financial plan. A financial plan keeps a couple accountable for their actions and focused on achieving dreams. It details goals and strategies for saving, spending, income and asset growth, debt reduction, insurance, estate planning, and taxes. It takes a couple's dreams and breaks them down into realistic steps. Thus, when certain financial milestones are achieved, it's truly a cause for celebration.

There are five financial planning principles: grow net worth through debt reduction and asset growth; set specific, measurable, attainable, realistic, and timely (SMART) goals; protect what you're building (with a will and insurance); implement your strategy; and evaluate your progress.

Learn about money management, dream big, and set goals. Respectful communication and teamwork keeps your relationship healthy and focused on achieving your dreams. And if you work together, you'll stay together. If you're stuck in a rut, get help; see an adviser or couple's counsellor.

TOO FAR GONE

There are instances when a relationship is too far gone, both personally and financially. Perhaps financial abuse is involved, or just an overall lack of personal and financial compatibility. Before you file divorce papers, try professional counselling. But don't kid yourself; this isn't a magic bullet that'll solve all your relationship issues. You have to be a smart and financially prudent young woman in the process. This may mean consulting with a lawyer simultaneously and knowing your rights.

SURROUND YOURSELF WITH SUPPORT

Beyond your intimate relationships, embarking on the journey toward improved financial health is way more fun when you have supportive people like friends or family members joining you. Talking and learning about money is a great way to spend your time together, and the outcome tends to be financially lucrative.

To spice things up with your close social network, why not start a money club with a few of your friends where you set financial goals and hold each other, and your personal spending plans, accountable. You could meet once a month over snacks and beverages to discuss your progress toward your goals, share tips, and help one another out when things get off track. Focus on a new theme each month, like automated banking, the best savings accounts, couponing, financial deal-breakers in relationships, or whatever. Heck — you could even discuss each of the chapters in this book. From time to time you may wish to host personal finance gurus like investment or insurance advisers. These experts can weigh in on some of your burning questions and provide advice.

The whole idea with forming a club is to help support one another and broaden everyone's financial knowledge.

GET A MONEY MENTOR

In addition to surrounding yourself with other financially savvy people, why not get a money mentor?

Ninety percent of young women receive money advice from their parents, if they receive any advice at all. Second to that, they ask their friends. Along the way we glean nuggets of financial information from people we trust. These are our money mentors, and it pays to have good ones.

My first money mentor was my mom — as you may remember from the introduction of this book, she helped me buy my first savings bond at age 10 with the $100 I'd received for my birthday. I got my first job at the local library when I was 14, and I met Ryan, my second money mentor. Ryan worked at my local bank; he introduced me to mutual funds and also gave me advice on how to save for university. Currently, my savvy aunt, a Toronto-based multi-millionaire interior designer, mentors me toward developing habits and behaviours of self-made millionaire women. According to her, not living how rich people "should" live and keeping what you've worked so hard to earn has made her rich.

Want a money mentor? Look for the following characteristics in money mentor candidates. First, they're rich! They've built their net worth steadily over time. Second, they keep and maintain a meticulous budget. Third, they are savvy spenders. Their motto is, "If you don't need it, don't buy it." Fourth, they'll take time to teach you their secrets and how to make more money in your career, save more, and invest wisely. They'll also help you set and refine your goals.

Look around you for a money mentor. Do you have a friend, family member, spirit guide, coworker, or someone else you admire who has these characteristics? If so, simply approach the person about the idea. To convince your prospective money mentor it's a good investment of her time, explain how you plan to prepare for the meetings (always have a specific agenda) and integrate your learning into your daily financial life. If she says no, perhaps she's strapped for time — ask if she could refer you to someone else. Often these people flock together, like birds of a feather.

By getting a money mentor to give you guidance, you can take your natural desire to create financial freedom for yourself, learn some technical financial skills, and implement them to build your net worth.

CONCLUSION

THE MORE YOU GIVE, THE MORE YOU GET

Building "richness" isn't about amassing a fortune; it's about having the freedom and financial means to achieve your goals and dreams. By aligning, balancing, and strengthening the three pillars of your personal, professional, and financial life, your future will be well-supported.

But this book wouldn't be complete without discussing the concept of giving. You'll recall from the first chapter that, along with savvy spending, saving for the future, and making more money, wealthy women cite "giving" as one of the key contributors to growing their wealth. And most of these self-made millionaire women didn't wait until they had oodles of money to start giving. They gave even when they had very little.

Giving money to a charity or volunteering is part of any solid financial plan; it feels great, saves money on taxes, and helps build wealth.

In addition, there is a return on your investment when you give of your time (volunteering), talent (skills), and treasure (money). The return comes in a variety of forms. Not only can you make a difference in your community, you'll benefit from leadership opportunities, expanded networks, job promotions, and business growth. The community of givers is large and powerful, and when you join it with wholesome intentions and dedication, the community will support and boost you up.

Wondering how to integrate giving into your financial plan? You don't need gobs of time or money to get started. Take a balanced approach. There are times in life when you'll have more time to give than money, or more skills and money to give than time. For example, for as far back as I can remember, I've been very passionate about uplifting women and girls through education, safe housing, health care, and more. So when I was through with university, and had very little money, I started volunteering my time at the local women's shelter. A few years later, when I had more professional experience (in finance), I joined the board of a national women's organization as their treasurer and became a financial donor.

Start by finding an organization that you care about. If you're not sure what charities you're interested in supporting, do a little soul searching. What are you passionate about? Ensuring children have affordable access to sports? Preserving and promoting local art? Providing financial-literacy education? Finding a cure for an illness that has impacted your family? Align your giving with an organization that represents your passions.

Then, determine how you can help. Perhaps the organization needs a new board member, or money and volunteer hours to build a new playground. If you plan to donate money, making automatic contributions from your bank account can make it easier from a budgeting perspective. And, like saving for your personal financial future, increase the amount you give away each year. If you're seriously strapped for cash but still want to contribute financially to a cause, ask friends and family to give money on your behalf to the organization, rather than give you gifts, for special occasions like birthdays, anniversaries, weddings, and other holidays.

Many self-made millionaire women target giving at least 10 percent of their income. But, giving is personal; how and how much you give can only be determined by you.

What I can guarantee, however, is if you really want professional, financial, and personal growth, give!

THE ROAD TO WELL-HEELED

You are well on your way to becoming a Well-Heeled and empowered young woman. As you invest your time, energy and money into improving your personal, professional, and financial life through hard work, savvy choices, pursuing your passions, and making positive contributions into the lives of others, you will create an awesome future for yourself — a future designed and paid for by you!

APPENDIX A

LADIES, TAKE THE 30-DAY FINANCIAL CHALLENGE

In closing, I want to challenge you — a talented and financially empowered young woman — to take the 30-day Financial Challenge. That's right, within 30 days you'll see immediate improvements to your cash flow and net worth. If you have a partner, take this challenge together.

Day 1: Come to grips with your current financial situation. This means coming clean with yourself, and your partner if you have one, about the condition of your finances. If you're up to your eyeballs in debt, you need to acknowledge it. If you've been a cheapskate, acknowledge it. Jot down the feelings you have about your financial status, what's working and what's not.

Days 2–5: Know where you stand financially so that you can create a plan to grow your bottom line. Download your favourite net-worth tracking tool to determine what you own and owe. All major banks have free online calculators, but if you want to build your own, simply total up your assets and subtract your liabilities. If you get lost, go through your stacks of mail and pull out all your financial statements. Lay each statement on your kitchen table, find the balance, and list it as either an asset or a liability.

Days 6–10: Set a SMART goal to increase your net worth each year. Remember, SMART financial goals are specific, measurable, attainable, realistic, and timely. If your net worth is currently $12,500, aim to increase it through debt reduction and asset growth to $20,000 by the end of next year. The following year, increase your net worth to $30,000, and so on. Again, with SMART goals, you'll need to put detailed plans in place to achieve them. If you get stuck, flip through the suggestions in this book again.

Again, hands down, the most effective ways to reduce debt are to make your payments automatically on the day you get paid, pay a little extra each month (even $10 makes a difference), and negotiate your interest rates so that you pay as little interest as possible.

The most effective ways to increase your assets are to save through tax-advantaged savings programs. If you've been sitting on the fence about home ownership, stop renting and build equity in your own home — but this only makes sense if your cash flow can handle it.

There are three surefire ways to erode your net worth: accumulating bad debt, spending your savings, and buying things you don't need.

Days 11–15: If you don't start tracking your money through budgeting, you'll lose it. According to author Dr. Thomas Stanley, the majority of self-made multi-millionaires keep meticulous budgets, even though they're rolling in dough. A terrific budgeting website is Mint.com, though you can download other free budgeting tools from any major bank. Ensure that you track your entire household's budget, even if you and your partner keep separate bank accounts.

Days 16–20: Review your budget and look for ways to cut back unnecessary expenses. Think about your food and shopping habits, and pay attention to the small expenses, as they can add up to be quite substantial. You'll want to take time to determine what are realistic budgeting goals. The keys with budgeting are to spend less than you make and prioritize savings and debt reduction through automatic payments. Remember, living a frugal life by minding your dollars and cents will help you accomplish your goals and motivate you to improve your financial health.

Days 21–25: Reduce your debt quickly by negotiating the lowest rates with your lenders. Call them up, ask for lower rates, present competitive offers, and if they don't want to co-operate, take your business elsewhere. Then plan to pay a little extra each month. This will help reduce the principal.

Day 26: Sign up for your company's retirement savings plan (it should take less than 30 minutes to enrol). Employers will often contribute free money. If you're self-employed, or your company doesn't have a plan, or even if they do but you want to save outside of their plan, sign up for a tax-advantaged retirement savings plan through any financial institution. Aim to tuck away 10–15 percent of your salary. If that's too steep, start with less and grow your contributions every six months.

Days 27–29: Meet with a qualified financial adviser and develop a plan to achieve your goals. To get started, think about where you want to be financially in 5–10 years. Does your life plan include travel, family, retirement, or a home purchase? Goal-setting is fun because you can dream about the future.

Day 30: From this day forward, commit to learning more about money by reading newspapers and books, speaking with professionals, and joining a supportive social network.

Lastly, while you build your bottom line, you still need to enjoy life and all of its experiences, which often cost money. Take a balanced approach to your 30-day Financial Challenge and the rest of your life!

Good luck! Go girl!

NOTES

CHAPTER 1

1. See Statistics Canada, consumer price index historical summaries: *www.statcan.gc.ca/tables-tableaux/sum-som/l01/cst01/econ46b-eng.htm*.

2. Several sources were consulted: Measuringworth.com; "Median and Average Sales Prices of New Homes Sold in United States," *www.census.gov/const/uspricemon.pdf*; Lalaine C. Delmendo, "U.S. House Price Rises Continue to Accelerate!" June 4, 2013, *www.globalpropertyguide.com*; Rob Carrick, "2012 vs. 1984: Young Adults Really Do Have It Harder Today," May 7, 2012, *www.theglobeandmail.com*; Trent Hamm, "It's Harder to Get Started Today," February 15, 2011, *www.thesimpledollar.com*.

3. U.S. Department Of Labor, Bureau of Labor Statistics, Washington, D.C., Consumer Price Index: *ftp://ftp.bls.gov/pub/special.requests/cpi/cpiai.txt*.

4. Julian Beltrame, Canadian Press, "Tuition Fees Ballooning in Canada: Report," September 11, 2012, *http://business.*

financialpost.com; National Center for Education Statistics, *http://nces.ed.gov/fastfacts/display.asp?id=76*; U.S. Inflation Calculator, *www.usinflationcalculator.com*.

CHAPTER 2

1. "Travel Reward Cards: Flights of Fancy and Points to Ponder," *CBC News, www.cbc.ca*.

CHAPTER 4

1. "The Debt of Nations," Zero Hedge.com, *www.zerohedge.com/news/2013-06-04/debt-nations*.
2. Two references were consulted: CGA Canada, "A Driving Force No More: Have Canadian Consumers Reached Their Limits?" *www.cga-canada.org*; CGA Canada, "Where is the Money Now: The State of Canadian Household Debt as Conditions for Economic Recovery Emerge," *www.cga-canada.org*.
3. Two references were consulted: Statistics Canada, "Population and private dwellings occupied by usual residents and inter-censal growth for Canada, 1971 to 2011", *www.statcan.gc.ca*; Statistics Canada, "Total Population in Canada, 2013", *www.statcan.gc.ca*.
4. Bertrand Marotte, "Canadian Consumer Debt Rises to $25,597, But Falls in Toronto and Vancouver," *Globe and Mail*, November 13, 2013, *www.theglobeandmail.com*.
5. Jonathan Spicer and Chizu Nomiyama (ed.), "U.S. Consumer Debt Drops in Second Quarter, Continuing Post-Crisis Trend," August 14, 2013, *www.reuters.com*.
6. Palash Ghosh, "Credit Card Debt In U.S.: Falling, But Still Very High," *International Business Times*, August 19, 2013, *www.ibtimes.com*.

7. TD Ameritrade, LearnVest and Business Wire, "Money and Marriage: How Finances Relate to Your Relationship", *mms. businesswire.com.*

8. Paul Ritz, "Did You Know Women Are Better At Handling Credit?" June 10, 2013, *www.nationaldebtrelief.com.*

9. Smart Money Chicks, "13 Scary Statistics about Women and Money," October 18, 2011, *http://smartmoneychicks.com.*

10. Two references were consulted: CGA Canada, "A Driving Force No More: Have Canadian Consumers Reached Their Limits?" *www.cga-canada.org*; CGA Canada, "Where is the Money Now: The State of Canadian Household Debt as Conditions for Economic Recovery Emerge," *www.cga-canada.org.*

11. Diana Olick, "Americans Are Tapping into Home Equity Again," February 8, 2013, *www.cnbc.com.*

CHAPTER 5

1. Conference Board of Canada, "Gender Income Gap," *www. conferenceboard.ca*; World Economic Forum, "The Global Gender Gap Report 2012," *www.weforum.org*; Meghan Casserly, "The Geography of the Gender Pay Gap: Women's Earnings By State," *Forbes, www.forbes.com.*

2. The U.S. Department of Labor and Census Bureau conducted a study in 2004 that suggested 75 percent of future North American jobs will require some type of post-secondary education. Additionally, they found that jobs requiring a bachelor's degree would grow twice as fast as the average for other occupations.

3. Robert Longley, "Lifetime Earnings Soar with Education: Master's Degree Worth $2.5 Million Income Over a Lifetime," updated August 17, 2013, U.S. Government Info, *usgovinfo. about.com.*

4. Two references were consulted: Statistics Canada, "Education and Occupation of High-Income Canadians," *www.statcan. gc.ca*; Benjamin Tal and Emanuella Enenajor, "Degrees of Success: The Payoff to Higher Education in Canada", August 26, 2013, CIBC World Markets, *www.cibcwm.com*.

5. "Women Entrepreneurs Are the Fastest Growing Segment of Business in America," *Kingdom Voices* magazine, *kingdomvoicesmag.com*.

6. RBC Canadian Women Entrepreneur Awards, *www.womenofinfluence.ca*.

CHAPTER 7

1. Financial Finesse Inc., "State of U.S. Employee Retirement Preparedness," *www.financialfinesse.com/wp-content/uploads/2013/09/2013_Retirement_Preparedness_Research_Report_FINAL.pdf*.

2. Steve Doughty, "Life Expectancy Gap Between Men and Women Narrows to Less than Four Years as Dorset Is Revealed as the Place to Grow Old," October 24, 2013, *www.dailymail.co.uk*.

3. Sham Gad, "Are Women's Portfolios Better than Men's?" August 22, 2012, *www.investopedia.com*.

CHAPTER 9

1. BMO Bank of Montreal, "BMO Financial Literacy Poll: 96 Per Cent of Canadians Believe Teaching Kids About Money Matters is Key to a Healthier Economy", *newsroom.bmo.com*.

2. Dr. Thomas Stanley, *Stop Acting Rich .... And Start Living Like a Real Millionaire* (Mississauga, ON: Wiley, 2011), Pages Preface xiii, 40, 204-205.

INDEX

ABOUT THE AUTHOR

Lesley-Anne Scorgie is the 30-year-old bestselling author of *Rich by Thirty: A Young Adult's Guide to Financial Success*, which has been published in English, French, and Korean. Her latest bestselling book, *Rich by Forty: A Young Couple's Guide to Building Net Worth*, focuses on giving young couples the skills to build their bottom line. Says the *Globe and Mail* of Lesley-Anne Scorgie: "[she is] wise beyond her years when it comes to spending and savings."

Lesley-Anne has made numerous television appearances including *The Oprah Winfrey Show*, *The Montel Williams Show*, *The Marilyn Denis Show*, and *MTV Live*. She is a regular columnist for *Metro News*. Her financial articles have appeared in publications such as *Men's Health* magazine, the *Globe and Mail*, the *Toronto Star*, *Unlimited* magazine, and the *Calgary Herald*. Lesley-Anne has been a spokesperson for Government Bonds and BMO Bank of Montreal.

In addition to owning and operating Rich By Inc., a financial consulting company dedicated to providing education, resources, and tools for a variety of demographics, Lesley-Anne also donates substantial time, energy, and resources to non-profits within her community. She is currently the treasurer for the National YWCA of Canada and is a member on the President's Think Tank Committee for the University of Alberta.

In 2011 Lesley-Anne won *Avenue Calgary*'s Top 40 Under 40 award and WXN's Top 100 Most Powerful Women in Canada award in the category of Future Leaders. She lives in Calgary, Alberta.

Follow Lesley-Anne Scorgie on Twitter: @LesleyScorgie and visit her website: *lesleyscorgie.com* for more common-sense tips about managing your finances.